E. M. Forster's Passages to India

V. Forster: Passage to India

E. M. Forster's Passages to India

ROBIN JARED LEWIS

New York   Columbia University Press

823
L

The Andrew W. Mellon Foundation, through a special grant, has assisted the Press in publishing this volume.

Library of Congress Cataloging in Publication Data

Lewis, Robin Jared.
   E. M. Forster's passages to India.

   Originated as the author's thesis, Columbia.
   Bibliography: p.
   Includes index.
   1. Forster, Edward Morgan, 1879–1970. A passage
to India. 2. Forster, Edward Morgan, 1879–1970—
Journeys—India. 3. India in literature. 4. India—
Description and travel—1901–1946. I. Title.
PR6011.058P3752   1979   823'.9'12   79-843
ISBN 0-231-04508-5

Columbia University Press
New York Guildford, Surrey

9 8 7 6 5 4 3 2

MLib

For NANCY

The thief of love has stolen my heart:
I am helpless with delight.

Contents

Preface

A great deal has been written on E. M. Forster's *A Passage to India*. It has been examined from an endless variety of viewpoints and, quite naturally, considerable emphasis has been placed upon the significance of India in Forster's book. Some critics have treated Forster's India as a metaphor for the complexity of human existence, while others have pointed to Indian metaphysical notions as being at the core of the work's meaning. A different approach has been to see the novel as Forster's admission of the failure of liberal humanism in the aftermath of the Great War. Those interested in the tradition of English fiction on India have offered yet another perspective by presenting Forster as heir to the legacy of Rudyard Kipling and Flora Annie Steel. All these aspects of Forster's novel are of genuine importance, yet a most significant area of inquiry has been largely ignored—the role of the author's personal experience of India in shaping his work.

Most of the primary material on Forster's time in India has been inaccessible, but the recent removal of restrictions for scholarly use has made large portions of the Forster archive at King's College, Cambridge available for the first time. The principal treasure in this collection is Forster's own diary of his first journey to India in 1912–13. This journal is not only an invaluable source for understanding his complex and passionate views on India: it is also a small masterpiece of the diarist's art, restrained, subtle, and evocative. I have quoted extensively from it in order to give the reader some idea of the intensity of Forster's first encounter with India, an intensity sufficient to inspire what many consider the finest book on India in English.[1]

The purpose of this study, then, is to trace Forster's involvement with India from its inception in 1906, when he met the young Syed Ross Masood at Oxford. This friendship eventually led to Forster's first Indian visit, from October 1912 to April 1913, during which he traveled extensively throughout north and central India. Since this journey was the one that spurred him to begin *A Passage to India,* I have discussed it in much greater detail than the others. The material at King's (which also includes the Indian diary of Forster's traveling companion Goldsworthy Lowes Dickinson) provides a solid basis for identifying locations, characters, and incidents in the novel that have their origins in the author's personal experience.

Forster's second Indian visit came in 1921, when he spent six months as Private Secretary to the Maharajah of Dewas Senior, a small princely state in central India. *The Hill of Devi* (1953) is a collection of Forster's letters and commentary from this period which I have used to illustrate the impact of this second visit upon the last section of the novel.

A third and final journey by Forster to India in 1945 had, of course, no effect on the making of the novel, but it did allow him to reestablish the ties of friendship and affection that meant so much to his life and work. Though these three passages to India are the focus of my study, I have also dealt with other periods of Forster's life when India occupied him in one way or another: for example, his acquaintance with Masood from 1906 to 1912, and the author's later years at Cambridge.

No matter which aspect of Forster's life is discussed, whenever possible I have let his own highly distinctive voice describe the personalities and situations involved. Forster's accounts of India and Indians show clearly that in writing *A Passage to India* he was very selective, lifting from personal experience only those elements that contributed to the novel's meaning. Life inevitably goes beyond art in these matters—the real person (Syed Ross Masood, for example) is far more complex and immediate than his fictional counterpart (Aziz)—so Forster simply took from experience what he needed and no more. In this sense, *A Passage to India* offers an intensely personal view of India under English rule, and Forster would have been the first to identify the book as such: he detested authors claiming to be purveyors of universal truths about "the real

India." A surprising number of the criticisms of the novel, from Indians and Westerners alike, have at their core the lament "I don't know what Forster can be thinking about. That's not *my* India—it's not the India *I* know." And indeed they are right: what is presented in *A Passage to India* is nothing more and nothing less than E. M. Forster's India. Therefore, the only intention of this book is to illuminate that particular India.

Although this study approaches *A Passage to India* primarily as a work of art, I hope that it also suggests indirectly the value of the novel as social history. One would certainly not want to take the book as the sole source for a portrait of social relations in British India early in this century. But as a corrective to and departure from the mainstream of Anglo-Indian[2] writing, it has considerable significance. The heroism, courage, and efficiency that characterized so many of the English in India had already been amply chronicled in fiction; until *A Passage to India,* however, their darker qualities had not. Forster's novel rejected the traditional stereotypes which formed the basis of Anglo-Indian fiction and replaced them with characters of recognizably human proportions. My hope is to show that this freshness of vision which has given the novel its high reputation originated in Forster's firsthand experience of India and its people.

I am extremely grateful to the Provost and Scholars of King's College, Cambridge for permission to quote from the unpublished material in the Forster archive at King's College Library and from Forster's many letters. Since they are the owners of the copyright of the Forster Papers, no part of this material may be reproduced without their permission. I particularly wish to thank the Twentieth Century Archivist at King's, Ms. Penelope Bulloch, for her generous guidance when I was there. I am grateful to Edward Arnold (Publishers) Ltd. for permission to quote from E. M. Forster's *A Passage to India.* Excerpts from E. M. Forster's *The Hill of Devi* and *Two Cheers for Democracy* are reprinted by permission of Harcourt Brace Jovanovich, Inc.; copyright 1951, 1953 by E. M. Forster. The quotations from the R. C. Trevelyan Papers appear with the kind permission of the Master and Fellows of Trinity College, Cambridge. I would also like to thank Trekkie Parsons, who graciously consented to my use of a quotation from one of Leonard Woolf's letters from Ceylon. Acknowledgment is also due to Begum Amtul Chhatari for permission to quote from the letters of E. M. Forster to her late husband Syed Ross Masood, and to Jalil A. Kidwai, the guardian of these letters, for his assistance. Santha Rama Rau (Mrs. Gurdon Wattles) has permitted me to quote from her personal papers, for which I am grateful. I also wish to thank Forster's biographer, P. N. Furbank, who has been most kind in taking time from his work to answer my many inquiries. The late Oliver Stallybrass, who was editing Forster's complete works, very kindly sent me advance proofs of the excellent textual and general notes for the new Abinger edition of *A Passage to India*.

My dear friend Ahmed Ali has helped me constantly over the past three years: he was my gracious host in Pakistan in 1976, and has corresponded ceaselessly to provide me with information. He has allowed me to quote from several letters of his from E. M. Forster, and, best of all, has shown me how kindness can be an inspiration in one's creative work.

Dr. W. G. Archer and Mildred Archer read the manuscript prior to publication and offered suggestions for its improvement. For this extremely generous assistance, I am especially grateful.

This book originated as a doctoral thesis at Columbia University, where I was given a Traveling Fellowship in 1975–76 that enabled me to conduct my research in India, Pakistan, and England. I was very fortunate in having the finest of advisers: in the English Department, Carolyn Heilbrun provided warm intellectual and personal support, and Carl Woodring offered invaluable guidance in the final stages of writing. Finally, Ainslie Embree gave me unlimited access to his vast store of knowledge about both England and India, but it is his quiet generosity and gentle friendship that I value most.

E. M. Forster's Passages to India

chapter 1

The Background of the First Visit

E. M. Forster's Early Years

In the biography of his great-aunt Marianne Thornton, E. M. Forster describes his own arrival into the world with a characteristic lightness of spirit, recording a comical mis-understanding between his father and the elderly verger at his christening:

> I was born at my parents' house, 6 Melcombe Place, Dorset Square, London, on January 1, 1879. Two months later I was taken down to Clapham to be christened, Miss Henrietta Synnot standing as my godmother. I had already been registered as Henry Morgan Forster, and that was to be my name. The party walked over from Aunt Monie's to the church on the Common. On the way the old verger asked my father what the baby was to be called, and he, distrait, gave his own name, Edward Morgan. This the verger wrote down upon a piece of paper. My maternal grand-mother held me at the font. When the clergyman asked her what I was to be called she became afraid of the sound of her voice in a sacred edifice, and indicated the piece of paper. My mother, in a distant pew, heard the announcement with horror. What on earth was to happen! It turned out after agitated research that the chris-tening had it, so Edward I am.[1]

The name Edward never stuck, however, for he soon be-came known to family and friends as Morgan, and so he re-mained throughout his long life. Yet the irony persists—that a man who valued order so much in his life and work should have started out in the midst of a muddle.

The author's nervous father was a young and promising architect whose mother was one of the nine children (six daughters and three sons) of Henry Thornton, a wealthy banker who was a mainstay of the famous Clapham Sect. The Thorntons had a proud tradition of social involvement—Henry Thornton's house Battersea Rise, located on the edge of Clapham Common, became the primary meeting place for the dynamic "brotherhood of Christian politicians"[2] which included William Wilberforce, Zachary Macaulay (father of the historian), Charles Grant, and James Stephen (great-grandfather of Virginia Woolf). In 1807, these pious Evangelicals helped effect the abolition of the slave trade in the colonies; six years later, they mounted a shrewd and successful crusade to rally British public opinion in favor of the opening up of India to Protestant missionaries. This last victory was to have a great impact on the future of British rule in India, for it marked the beginning of a steady conversion of the Raj from a commercial enterprise to a moral and social mission. Whereas in the eighteenth century the central consideration had been the profit margin of the East India Company, from 1813 the focus shifted with ever-increasing intensity to the reform of Indian society, to cleaning up what Charles Grant called "the offal of Hindoo morals."[3] Forster admired the moral earnestness of his ancestors, but he was at times cynical about the missionary movement, ascribing part of its success to the overflow of mid-Victorian prosperity:

> Much unselfishness and heroism went to the growth of Missions, but they also met a home need. There was surplus money in England, seeking a sentimental outlet. Some societies would have endowed art and literature with the surplus: our middle class spent theirs in trying to alter the opinions and habits of people whom they had not seen.[4]

The rigid purposefulness that Forster inherited from his father's side, however, was tempered by the very different qualities of his mother's family. Alice Clara Whichelo (known as Lily), Forster's mother, was the daughter of an impecunious drawing master who died young, leaving a widow and ten children to fend for themselves. The boys were sent to work as clerks, the girls as governesses; and the Whichelos' life of genteel impoverishment produced attitudes understandably different from the piety and earnest optimism of the Thorntons. Forster says of his mother's family: "They had no enthusiasm for work, they were devoid of the public spirit, and they were averse to piety and quick to detect the falsity sometimes accompanying it."[5]

His father died suddenly when Forster was only a small baby: it was therefore his mother who guided his childhood, and she continued this tradition of cant-free bluntness in bringing up her son. He always emphasized in later years the great influence that her common-sensical attitudes had had on him:

> My father (the son of a clergyman) died early, and my mother retired with me into the country and provided me with a sheltered and happy childhood. Religion had its place: we were Church of England and she read morning prayers to the two maids and me, but she was never intense, and I suspect not very attentive. Her interests lay elsewhere: in helping her neighbors: in running her little house and garden: in district visiting: and in criticising Queen Victoria's Jubilee. The middle classes kow-towed to Royalty much less than they do now. They were not under the continuously dripping tap of the B.B.C. which has done so much to sodden rebellion. My mother, generally so retiring, once rose up at a public meeting where it was suggested that everyone, however poor, should give the dear Queen one penny, and said she wouldn't.[6]

The house to which Forster and his mother "retired" in 1883 was Rooksnest, near Stevenage in Hertfordshire, and it was here that he acquired his great love for the English countryside. Forster always spoke of his early childhood in Hertfordshire with a genuine warmth and affection untainted by sentimentality, and Rooksnest provided the model for Howards End, a house which embodied for him the continuity of generations of English yeomanry. Speaking of his childhood to an Italian audience in 1959, Forster, then eighty years old, described Rooksnest in subdued but glowing terms that reveal how deeply he still felt about it:

> I went to live in the English countryside when I was four. It was quiet agricultural country—Hertfordshire—and though it was only thirty miles from the metropolis it seemed at the ends of the

earth. Our house—a small brick one—may once have been a farm
and at the end of the garden was an actual farm, large and strag-
gling. The fields sloped Westward into a tremendous view. A little
lane connected us with civilization—in the winter it was impass-
able with mud. Overhanging the house was an enormous wych
elm and in its bark some white pigs' teeth had been stuck. Yes
pigs' teeth. They had been stuck in as a superstitious preventative
against toothache. People would come and chew the bark and so
obtain alleviation from their pangs. This had stopped in my day,
and presently the bark grew over the teeth and hid them and finally the tree was cut down. But the house it overshadowed with
its primitive magic still stands, and some of you may have guessed
the house is Howards End.

Those early years made a deep impression which no amount
of suburbanism or travel has dispelled. When I think of England it
is of the countryside, and I still think of her thus though so little of
our countryside remains.[7]

Forster wrote that as a boy he had hoped to live and die in
Rooksnest,[8] but when he was fourteen, his mother sold the
house. She took her unwilling son to live in Tunbridge Wells,
having entered him as a day boy at the Tonbridge School in
nearby Tonbridge. He seems to have hated his public school almost at once. The regimentation, the false camaraderie, and the
reactionary social outlook all left their mark on his spirit and led
him to write feelingly of the unhappy plight of a harried day boy
at "Sawston School" in *The Longest Journey*. As John Colmer
has pointed out, Forster always spoke of this novel as one into
which he had put many of his own experiences, and thus it is
fair to consider the account of Sawston as "thinly veiled autobiography."[9] Forster's essay "Notes on the English Character"
contains his most incisive comments on the English public
school system and on the men it produces, men who appear so
frequently in his novels. Herbert Pembroke in *The Longest
Journey*, Henry Wilcox in *Howards End,* and Ronny Heaslop in
A Passage to India are examples of a peculiarly English inability
to feel, which Forster attributes to the narrow and inhuman
value system of the public schools:

they go forth into a world that is not entirely composed of public-
school men or even of Anglo-Saxons, but of men who are as

various as the sands of the sea; into a world of whose richness and subtlety they have no conception. They go forth into it with well-developed bodies, fairly developed minds, and undeveloped hearts. And it is this undeveloped heart that is largely responsible for the difficulties of Englishmen abroad.[10]

Forster's unhappiness at public school was shared by many of his acquaintances, among them Goldsworthy Lowes Dickinson, his teacher at Cambridge and later an intimate friend. In his biography of Dickinson, Forster writes of the initial bewilderment that both men had felt upon coming up to Cambridge for the first time:

> He [Dickinson] had no idea what Cambridge meant—and I remember having the same lack of comprehension about the place myself, when my own turn came to go up there. It seems too good to be real. That the public school is not infinite and eternal, that there is something more compelling in life than teamwork and more vital than cricket, that firmness, self-complacency and fatuity do not between them compose the whole armour of man, that lessons may have to do with leisure, and grammar with literature—it is difficult for an inexperienced boy to grasp truths so revolutionary, or to realize that freedom can sometimes be gained by walking out through an open door. The door had been opened before, to be closed.[11]

Cambridge was thus a sudden and unexpected liberation for Forster—it gave him values to replace those which had so repelled him at Tonbridge and brought him into contact for the first time with the best English intellectual traditions, which he later characterized as "the fearless uninfluential Cambridge that sought for reality and cared for truth."[12]

Entering Cambridge in 1897 to read Classics, Forster spent four happy years at King's College; he took a Second Class in 1900 and then stayed an additional year reading History, in which he also received a Second. His history tutor was the infamous Oscar Browning, an outrageous eccentric who sometimes listened to essays in his bath, or, when he deigned to show up at his office, with a red handkerchief over his face. But a much more important influence was Forster's Classics tutor, Nathaniel Wedd, whom he described as "cynical, aggressive,

Mephistophelian." [13] Wedd ignited Forster's passion for ancient Greece and also introduced him to modern authors then considered beyond the pale of literary study—Ibsen, Zola, George Moore, and Shaw. Wedd was also violently antireligious, and his biting remarks about Christianity became legend at King's. On one occasion when the meat in Hall was particularly tough, he is said to have exclaimed in pugnaciously loud tones, "Why, this lamb is almost as hard to swallow as the Lamb of God!" [14]

Neither Wedd nor Browning, however, had quite the impact on Forster as did his election in 1899 to the Cambridge Conversazione Society, better known as the Society of the Apostles. This was a private discussion group founded in the 1820s that had attained great prominence in intellectual circles by the time Forster was an undergraduate: among the dons and fellows who were members at the turn of the century were Alfred North Whitehead, Goldsworthy Lowes Dickinson, Roger Fry, J. M. E. McTaggart, G. E. Moore, and Bertrand Russell. Forster's fellow undergraduate Apostles included John Maynard Keynes, Lytton Strachey, R. C. Trevelyan, Desmond Mac-Carthy, and Leonard Woolf. This extraordinary collection of men gathered every Saturday evening during the term to hear a member's paper read aloud, after which a lively discussion ensued. In this atmosphere of passionate intellectualism tempered with irreverent humor, Forster found a spiritual home which embodied for him the perfect harmony between ideas and individuals:

> As Cambridge filled up with friends it acquired a magic quality. Body and spirit, reason and emotion, work and play, architecture and scenery, laughter and seriousness, life and art—these pairs which are elsewhere contrasted were there fused into one. People and books re-inforced one another, intelligence joined hands with affection, speculation became passion, and discussion was made profound by love. [15]

Spurred on by a diffident comment from Wedd ("I don't see why you should not write") [16] and drawing on the intellectual self-confidence that he had gained from his apostleship, Forster began writing for several undergraduate magazines. When he left Cambridge in 1901, he spent a year in Italy, and this experience provided the inspiration not only for his first half-dozen published short stories but also for his two "Italian novels," *Where Angels Fear to Tread* (1905) and *A Room with a View* (1908). Between 1901 and 1910, Forster traveled extensively on the Continent, constantly collecting varied impressions to add substance to his writing. Italy and Greece remained his favorite countries, and this preference is reflected in the preponderance of classical settings in his novels and short stories of the period.

Friendship with Syed Ross Masood

By 1910, however, Forster was restless; he wanted to go beyond the familiar confines of the Mediterranean, to escape the hothouse atmosphere of European culture, and the opportunity came when he was invited to visit India by his friend Syed Ross Masood. Writing in 1959, Forster outlined the circumstances that led to his first Indian visit:

> My connection with India is peculiar and personal. It started because I made friends with an Indian, and but for him I might never have gone to the country, or written about it. His name was Masood, he was a Moslem, who had come over to go to Oxford; we saw a great deal of each other and travelled in Italy and France and when he returned to India it was agreed that I should go to stay with him. This I did in 1912, and twelve years later when *A Passage to India* came out I dedicated it to him.[17]

Forster's friendship with Masood was a long and affectionate one, lasting until the latter's death in 1937, and in writing *A Passage to India* Forster drew upon his intimate friendship with Masood to create the character of Aziz.

Syed Ross Masood had come to England in 1906 bearing the rather awesome mantle of his famous grandfather, Sir Syed Ahmad Khan, the man whom many historians consider the virtual savior of the Indian Muslim community in the late nine-

teenth century. A fearless intellectual and aggressive social reformer, Sir Syed had achieved his greatest success in the
founding in 1875 of the Muhammadan Anglo-Oriental College
at Aligarh:[18] this institution had redirected the energies of the
moribund Muslim upper classes toward educating themselves
in order to claim their share of the benefits of British rule. Sir
Syed's unique amalgam of traditional Muslim ideas and liberal
Western values provided a positive ideology to replace the self-
destructive and melancholic nostalgia for lost glories among Indian Muslims after the final snuffing out of the Mughal Empire
in 1857.

Under Syed Ahmad Khan's determined leadership, Aligarh
became the center of this new movement (usually known as
"the Muslim Revival"),[19] and when his first and only grandson
was born in 1889, Sir Syed was determined that the boy be
recruited at an early age to carry on his own work of revitalizing
Muslim life in India. When Syed Ross Masood reached the age
of four years and four months in 1893, his grandfather executed
an elaborate piece of showmanship by arranging for the boy's
bismillah ceremony to take place as part of the official agenda of
the eighth annual meeting of the prestigious Muhammadan Educational Conference at Aligarh.[20] This ceremony, the first important one in the life of a male Muslim child, is usually an in-
trafamily event at which the boy is taught the opening lines of
the Koran in order to set him firmly on the path of Islamic piety.
By making a traditionally private event into a boldly public one,
Sir Syed was declaring in no uncertain terms to the often skep-
tical Muslim elite that his fight for reform would be carried on
by future generations. As a further departure from orthodoxy,
he placed the customary five hundred rupees' gift in front of the
young Masood and asked, "What should be done with this
money?", to which the boy replied unflinchingly, "Give it to the
college."[21]

In this invigorating but rather solemn atmosphere, the
young Syed Ross Masood was raised. His father was a distinguished Cambridge-educated jurist, Syed Mahmood,[22] who rose
to a post on the High Court, one of only three Indians to do so at
the time.[23] But since Justice Mahmood was often away at Alla-

habad, where the High Court sat, Masood's childhood at Aligarh was spent largely under the watchful eye of his august grandfather, who carefully groomed him to carry on his inherited responsibilities as an adult.

Sir Syed Ahmad Khan died in 1898, and Masood's father died shortly afterwards, in 1903; in accordance with Sir Syed's wishes, Masood, now a handsome fourteen-year-old, was placed under the guardianship of Sir Theodore Morison, then Principal of the Muhammadan Anglo-Oriental College. Morison was a Cambridge graduate who had gone directly from the university to India, where he served for several years as tutor to a young Hindu prince, the Maharajah of Chhatarpur: when Forster visited India in 1912, he carried an introduction from Morison to Chhatarpur which led to a long and close friendship with the ruler of this tiny state in the center of the subcontinent.[24] In 1886, while visiting some Cambridge friends who were teaching at Aligarh, Morison met Sir Syed Ahmad Khan and was talked into coming to the college to serve as professor of history, which he did in 1889. He became Principal in 1899 and remained until 1905, when he returned to England as a new member of the India Council (under the aegis of the Secretary of State for India).[25] In 1906, Morison sent for Masood to come to England in order that the young man might be tutored in several subjects prior to entering Oxford the following year. One of the subjects was Latin, and the tutor that Morison engaged was E. M. Forster. This marked the beginning of an enduring and fruitful relationship of over thirty years, punctuated by several visits in both directions between England and India.

Masood went up to Oxford in 1907, and he remained at New College until 1911, when he received a Second Class in History.[26] His Oxford career was largely a happy one, and his contemporaries remembered him above all for his captivatingly warm personality. The distinguished historian H. A. L. Fisher, who was Masood's tutor and later became Warden of New College, remembered his pupil as an all-around success:

> My friend Sir Syed Ross Masood, who took his degree from New College in 1907 [sic], was a remarkable figure during his undergraduate life. His fine appearance, brilliant conversation, warm

sympathies, and eminence on the lawn tennis field brought him a
large number of friends and admirers.

He was, in fact, one of the most popular and successful undergraduate members of the College, and although my memory now
goes back over many years, I cannot recall the name of any young
Indian who has entered more thoroughly into the life of Oxford, or
has obtained from Oxford more of the best which Oxford has to
give.[27]

A more detailed glimpse of Masood's time in England is offered by his letters from Forster during the years 1907 to 1912:
in them one can see the gradual development of a frank and affectionate relationship that became vital to the lives of both
men.[28] The earliest letter, dated 21 April 1907, begins and ends
rather formally ("Dear Masood" and "Yours ever, E. M. Forster") and is taken up with the mundane business of thanking
Masood for a gift of some shoes. Forster manages to do this with
considerable charm:

As I write I wear your shoes! They are even more beautiful than I
expected and make my socks, and indeed the whole of me, look
horribly dowdy and prosaic. Thank you so much—both for them
and for all the trouble you have taken in getting them: on both accounts I value them greatly.[29]

A year later, after a prolonged visit by Masood to Forster's home
in Weybridge during the summer holidays, Forster's tone has
altered somewhat: in this letter he passes from an amusing
anecdote about a grim dinner party to a clear expression of affection. Having enquired briefly about Masood's holiday in
France, he writes:

I will now change back again, from you to me, or rather to us
both which is the best subject of all. I miss you very much. There
is no one whom I care about in Weybridge, and I can't tell you how
nice it was to have you coming in, and always to be dropping in on
you.[30]

Subsequent letters, written in late 1908 and throughout
1909, show that the subject of personal relations, so central to
Forster's work, was incessantly discussed by the two friends,
sometimes lightly, at other times in more solemn tones. During

an exchange reminiscent of the bantering between Aziz and Fielding in *A Passage to India,* Forster replies sarcastically to Masood's complaint that his letters are too perfunctory:

> Dear Masood
>
> What am I to write about? All the usual topics are barred. I mayn't say "thank you for my pleasant/beastly visit," nor for "the beautiful/stupid book that you so kindly/unkindly gave me when I was lucky/unlucky enough to be in your delightful/godforsaken room." For if I do, you will fly into a passion and cry that I'm being formal. Well, make up a polite message for yourself. I'm hanged if I'll bother myself. After your welcome/intrusive appearance at Oxford station, I travelled away comfortably home, and met my cousin at Weybridge.[31]

A growing informality appears in the opening to a letter written soon afterward, and the gentle chaffing about social forms continues:

> Masood, you're a beast. You say you've lots to tell me and it turns out to be "thank" on one page and "you" on the other. I don't call that a letter—it's a verbal exercise, and let me have no more such.[32]

By the end of 1909, further social conventions have been breached: Forster now signs his letters "Yours ever, EMF," and immediately successive letters begin "Dearest boy" and close with "Yours with love, EMF" or "Your affectionate EMF." A letter written to Masood while he was in France contains more echoes of Aziz and Fielding and discloses a new level of intimacy in their friendship, referring to a poem Masood wrote for Forster:

> We musn't quarrel about sentiment. We agree that it's the greatest thing in the world, and only differ as to how it's to be made the most of, and while I was reading your letter I didn't even differ. Who wrote "Each time that thou goest out of my sight—?" It's very beautiful.[33]

Perhaps the most revealing instance of the absolute understanding that had developed between Forster and Masood comes in a letter written in January of 1910. Here we can see that Forster feels close enough to Masood to make a joke along racial lines that would have been totally out of the question in most other interracial relationships, even in the urbane and sophisticated world of Oxford and Cambridge:

> Good night again,
> from Forster, member of the Ruling Race
> to Masood, a nigger.
> And let the latter buck up and write. And let him have a good time at Oxford. And let him and all his be happy. Otherwise:
> Forster will never travel in the same railway carriage with him again.[34]

These letters reveal the unusually relaxed tenor of the friendship: indeed, Masood's lack of touchiness on racial matters was considered by Forster to be one of his friend's most endearing qualities. The tone of sardonic amusement at Indo-British social tensions which pervades parts of *A Passage to India* may be attributed in some measure to Forster's admiration for Masood's casual attitude toward social insults. After Masood's death in 1937, Forster would write of him:

> Leaving aside his English friends, whom he placed in a class apart, what did he feel about the Ruling Race as a whole? Perhaps his private thoughts are best expressed in a remark which has always amused me: "As for your damned countrymen, I pity the poor fellows from the bottom of my heart, and give them all the help I can." He was irritated by the English, he was sometimes bitter about them, but he realised that they were awkwardly placed in India, and he extended, half humourously, his sympathy towards them in their plight.[35]

Plans for the First Visit

Before meeting Masood, Forster had had virtually no contact with India or things Indian, but this new and different acquaintance stirred his curiosity and opened up the prospect of a possible visit. From the narrow confines of Forster's "suburban and academic life" (as he himself described it),[36] India appeared, as it did to most Britons, "a vague jumble of rajahs, sahibs, babus, and elephants."[37] Masood was able to make this exotic figment of the popular imagination into something much more real—and therefore more interesting. As Masood's Oxford career drew to a close and he began preparations for his return to India, he urged Forster to consider following him out for a visit. The obvious obstacle was a financial one, but the unexpected and immediate success of Forster's novel *Howards End*, which appeared in October of 1910, suddenly made the journey distinctly possible. Forster breached the subject to Masood in a letter written a month after the publication of his new novel:

> I must tell you one more thing. My book is selling so well that I shall probably make enough money by it to come to India. There will not only be an American edition, but a Canadian, and perhaps a translation into French. I do not tell most people this because they would think I was bragging, but I know that you will understand, and feel what I feel.[38]

Forster soon immersed himself in reading about India to prepare for the upcoming journey. Two letters from early 1911 indicate the enthusiasm with which he read and the variety of perspectives he sought to understand:

> I am reading Lyall's hard book about the English in India— the sort of thing I required. Also failed to read another of Alice Perrin's novels called *Idolatry*. The other I tried was good, but this is about missionaries and wicked Hindus, and most tiresome.[39]

> What do you think I have been reading, and with great interest? You will never guess: the life of your grandfather. Of course a good deal of it is beyond me, but the chapters on his journey to England have filled me with admiration and pleasure. I shall send the book on to my aunt. I have finished Lyall's British Conquest of India, or whatever it is called, and am now tackling his Asiatic Studies, which I find abstruse, but full of great beauties of style. India, you see, is already occupying me.[40]

In 1912, Masood returned to India to begin his short-lived practice as a barrister at Patna, a city on the Ganges between

Calcutta and Benares,[41] and several months later, in October of 1912, Forster embarked by ship from Naples to join him, accompanied by several friends from his Cambridge days. Thus began the first of Forster's three passages to India and a lifelong fascination with its people.

chapter 2

First Passage:
British India, 1912–13

The Voyage Out

E. M. Forster embarked from Naples on October 7, 1912 amid the confusion and bustle that inevitably accompanied journeys to India by ship. He was traveling with his friend Robert Trevelyan, a poet who had been at Trinity College, Cambridge when Forster was at King's; three days later, at Port Said, they were joined by Goldsworthy Lowes Dickinson, Forster's Cambridge mentor.[1] Dickinson had been awarded an Albert Kahn Travelling Fellowship, the gift of a wealthy French Jew who believed in fostering world peace through an understanding of foreign cultures. "The Don," as the youthful officers he met at Peshawar called Dickinson, was to visit India, China, and Japan in the interests of international harmony.[2]

Forster's initial entries in his personal diary are taken up with delightful descriptions of the Italian coast and the "fine violet seas,"[3] but in the end his fatigue overtakes him: "Too much gab today. Hardly a moment to think that I am going to India."[4] Nearly twenty years later, Forster recalled that his fondest memories of the voyage stemmed from the beauty of the sea:

> We hated the boat, but the voyage to Bombay was fascinating
> I have been that way since, but have never again seen such colours in the sea, so many flying fish, dolphins and sharks, such sunsets, such flights of birds and of butterflies (the last-named meeting us when we were still two days from the Indian coast).[5]

Forster was disenchanted with his fellow-passengers, a tiresome collection of Anglo-Indians who found the three Cambridge intellectuals unspeakably amusing and dubbed them

"The Professors" or "The Salon."[6] This was Forster's first contact with narrow Anglo-Indian society, and it is reasonable to
surmise that some of the lessons of racial etiquette he learned
on the ship remained in his mind when he sat down to write his
Indian novel. Dickinson shared Forster's distaste for their traveling companions, remarking caustically in his autobiography
that "the company was one not naturally congenial to me."[7]
Both men mention in their diaries the refusal of the Anglo-Indians to have anything to do with a young Indian on board who
was bound home after several years in a British public school.
Forster recorded a comment that exemplifies the fear and re-
sentment so many Anglo-Indians felt for Indians: "Lady neigh-
bour: 'They tell me that young Indian's lonely. I say well he
ought to be. They won't let us know their wives, why should we
know them? If we're pleasant to them, they only despise us."[8]
Dickinson met the same woman soon after and acidly referred
to her in his diary as "Forster's lady—who thinks the boycotting
perfectly right and is much concerned with Anglican religion."[9]
Forster was also dismayed by the petty treatment of the young
Indian, who was even ostracized in deck games:

> Played the shovel-board tournament and spoilt the chances of
> a promising partner, who was nice over it. Horrid female opponent.
> By what selection are the organisers of these things found? As if
> by magic the appropriate colonel or captain is at the top. And is it
> chance that the Indian has been drawn to play with the wife of his
> guardian, believed a semi-Indian? This fetish of the ladies! And
> they are worth so little.[10]

Forster and Dickinson were also subjected to the usual
Anglo-Indian tirades about the "grandmotherly"[11] actions of the
British government in India. Anglo-Indians with even minimal
experience in India fancied themselves experts on "the native
question," and they often echoed the sentiments of one Captain
Baker, who confided to Dickinson that the proper attitude was
"survival of the fittest, fighting force with force."[12] Dickinson
describes another conversation of the same nature, this with an
Anglo-Indian returning from home leave:

> Conversation with medical service man (?army). Down on Curzon
> for initiating a fresh trial of Englishman acquitted for insulting In-

dians—general grumbling that Indians are getting the best of it—in the old days you could flog a man without any report—now must write a full report. . . .[13]

These sentiments were largely characteristic of Anglo-Indian opinion in 1912, a time when nationalist agitation was beginning to worry even the most blusteringly confident of "old India hands." As one historian has pointed out, many of the English saw Indians as children and drew the obvious conclusion: "In an age when 'sparing the rod' was the equivalent of 'spoiling the child' it is obvious that relations with a people considered to be children would involve a large degree of force." [14]

Another way of dealing with the complexities and contradictions of a life of exile in India was to pretend that Indians didn't exist, a mental habit that many Anglo-Indians cultivated assiduously. Forster's close friend Joe Ackerley recalls a conversation he had that illustrates this:

> "Do you like India?" Mrs. Bristow asked me.
> "Oh yes. I think it's marvelous."
> "And what do you think of the people?"
> "I like them very much, and think them most interesting."
> "Oo, aren't you a fibber! What was it you said the other day about 'awful Anglo-Indian chatter'?"
> "But I thought you were speaking of the Indians just now, not the Anglo-Indians."
> "The Indians! I never think of them."
> "Well, you said 'the people,' you know."
> "I meant *us* people, stupid!"
> "I see. Well now, let's start again." [15]

This type of denial was widespread, and was often all the more insidious because it was expressed in tones of genteel boredom, of suave and worldly indifference. Sensitive visitors like Forster, Dickinson, and Ackerley were driven to distraction by this mannered diffidence, as were the few Anglo-Indians, like Sir Henry Cotton, who were receptive to Indian aspirations. Cotton served nearly four decades in the Indian Civil Service and came in 1907 to the sad conclusion that his countrymen had failed to respond to their environment in any real sense:

> The attitude of Anglo-Indians is an indication of the unsympathetic relations which exist between the two races. For the most

part it is an attitude of complete indifference. Englishmen in India
are blind to the real and obvious meaning of the great changes
which are taking place before their eyes. They know not the ma-
chinery which works the change, and they see not the change itself. They live and behave, as far as possible, as though they were
not in India at all.[16]

There was only one fellow passenger that Forster and Dickinson found at all congenial, a young officer named Searight
who had, in Dickinson's words, "literary ambitions"[17] and who
proved to be a welcome relief from the strident racism of the
other passengers. An insight into Forster's character is gained
by comparing his initial reason for noticing Searight to Dickinson's. The older man was fascinated with the young soldier's
flamboyant demeanor, but Forster simply notes in his diary, "I
like him. He is good to the little Indian."[18] In Dickinson's autobiography, published posthumously in 1973, there is a more
frank picture of Searight:

> we discovered one interesting figure, a young officer called
> Searight, of a romantic Byronic temperament, homosexual and
> perpetually in love with some boy or other, with a passion for liter-
> ature, and writing an autobiography of which he showed us parts,
> in a style which also seemed to belong to Byron—not good, I sup-
> pose, but curiously moving.[19]

One can easily picture the natural and relaxed friendship that
sprang up between the three men, all literary, all homosexual,
and all alienated by the pugnacious philistinism of the other
passengers. Before disembarking at Bombay, Searight extended
a warm invitation to visit his regiment at Peshawar on the fabled Northwest Frontier: this experience was later to prove Forster's only contact with military life in India.[20]

Forster's voyage out to India provided him with his first
sour taste of Anglo-Indian society, and it gave him an inkling
that, whatever he might make of India itself, he was not one of
"the herd,"[21] as he later called the English in A Passage to
India. He was unwilling to subscribe to the idea of rigid solidarity with "one's own kind," a solidarity broken in the novel both
by Mrs. Moore, who openly criticizes a countrywoman to Aziz at

their first meeting in the mosque, and by Fielding, who resists the communal hysteria when Aziz is arrested. But Forster never shut himself off from individual Anglo-Indians: during his travels he made several new and satisfying friendships with sympathetic and intelligent Anglo-Indians who had rejected the conventional prejudices of their community.

First Impressions: Bombay

Forster's first sight of India was, appropriately enough, an illusion: what seemed to be the shoreline was only a cloud. The diary entry that records his arrival in Bombay brings to mind the uneasy atmosphere of Mrs. Moore's departure from the same harbor in the novel. In describing his first moments in India, Forster's prose is terse but evocative:

> Oct. 22   False India—a cloud bank—turned into true, a queer red series of hills, a little disquieting, as though Italy had been touched into the sinister. I had seen little yellow butterflies the day before, and now other kinds fluttered among the baggage. The Taj hotel was the most prominent building—our destination, but a rumour of cholera came. The last horrid meal on the horrid ship ended as we reached Bombay, and we went on shore in style in a native boat, an ugly crew but beautiful skins.[22]

Except for a very few travelers who reached India by the overland route, Bombay was the usual point of entry for the English in 1912, and as such it inevitably seemed to new arrivals a queer amalgam of English and Indian culture. Forster too felt an initial confusion with this city which, as he put it in *A Passage to India,* "the West had built and abandoned with a gesture of despair."[23] His diary contains a single, jumbled entry on this bustling city:

> Bombay. The English have built it and filled it with modern toys, and have gone away leaving the Indians to play there. Trams, Gothic architecture; Army and Navy Stores have little black chil-

dren with lolling eyes to watch the purchasers; a sleeper crouched outside the sweep of the Taj Hotel. We dashed about it in flies and saw Luce off in the evening.[24]

Forster's first stay in Bombay lasted barely two days, but it did serve to introduce him to a particularly troublesome cross-cultural relationship: master and servant. English memoirs of India are pervaded by a continuing sense of frustration at the failure of the Ruling Race to understand Indian servants. Forster encountered this difficulty almost immediately upon arriving in India:

> The first man to speak to me was the servant—but I will not dwell on my folly. Suffice that I accepted him, forgot his face, rejected him when he slept at my door in the hotel, and spent this day and the next in hunting for him.[25]

Dickinson and Trevelyan, who were leaving Forster for a few days in order to see the caves at Ajanta and Ellora,[26] fared no better in this respect. Forster writes:

> Then we parted for a time, Dickinson and Bob Trevelyan going off with a deplorable servant called Samuel, whom they shared, and who wailed "This is no proper arrangement" as soon as he had to do any work. They took turns controlling Samuel.[27]

Forster may well have had Samuel in mind when he created Anthony, the Goan Christian servant of Adela Quested and Mrs. Moore:

> The ladies' servant stood apart, with a sneering expression on his face. They had hired him while they were still globe-trotters in Bombay. In a hotel or among smart people, he was excellent, but as soon as they consorted with anyone whom he thought second-rate he left them to their disgrace.[28]

Many Anglo-Indian authors have noted the complex role-playing that master-servant relationships encouraged, and though the predominant tone of most writers is one of bewilderment and incomprehension, there are those who emphasize the genuine affection that sometimes arose in the face of formidable social barriers. One of the things that Forster found most attractive about Indian society was its latitudinarian quality, which allowed for an endless variety of personal relationships, even in

situations with an obvious potential for hostility. As Edmund
Candler put it:

> The old-fashioned type of Indian servant of happy traditions, who
> knows how to endear himself to his master, has few equals. He
> needs discovering, but the good sahib will find him, or perhaps
> create him, if he bides his time. Someday he will have a greybeard
> to wait on him, who will combine the presence and dignity of
> Abraham with a tender sensitiveness to his master's well being. In
> the mind of this picturesque and devoted attendant the sahib's
> relationship of ma-bap [mother-and-father] is really no fiction, for
> the Indian servant is something more than an actor. He becomes
> the part he has assumed by living it and believing it. When the
> arts of affiliation become instinctive they are no longer arts. Real
> smiles and tears of welcome and distress mark the sahib's coming
> and going, and the sahib himself is heavy of heart when the day of
> separation comes.[29]

The proverbial contempt of Anglo-Indians for servants must,
however, be considered the norm, and Forster epitomizes this in
Mrs. Turton, of whose Urdu language skills he writes, "She had
learnt the lingo, but only to speak to her servants, so she knew
none of the politer forms and of the verbs only the imperative
mood."[30] Even those who made a real effort to be friendly and
polite were often discouraged by their fellow Anglo-Indians, as
in the case of one woman whose husband admonished her,
"You needn't grin at them so affably, . . . they will only think
you are weak in the head."[31]

Forster soon learned the peculiar etiquette of harmonious
master-servant relations, and this understanding is expressed
early in A Passage to India, when Hamidullah interrupts a conversation with his guests to inquire about the evening meal:
"He raised his voice suddenly, and shouted for dinner. Servants
shouted back that it was ready. They meant that they wished it
was ready, and were so understood, for nobody moved."[32] Both
Hamidullah and his servants are playing their accepted roles in
this scene, as is Ronny Heaslop when his office peon, ironically
named Krishna, cannot be found:

> Ronny stormed, shouted, howled, and only the experienced ob-
> server could tell that he was not angry, did not much want the
> files, and only made a row because it was the custom. Servants,

quite understanding, ran slowly in circles, carrying hurricane
lamps. Krishna the earth, Krishna the stars replied, until the Englishman was appeased by their echoes, fined the absent peon
eight annas, and sat down to his arrears in the next room.[33]

Another strong initial impression that Forster gained from
his first few days in India was an aesthetic one: not the usual
admiration for Mughal architecture or Rajput miniatures, but a
powerful sense of the beauty of human forms amid the startling
vistas of rural India. Leaving Bombay by train for some sightseeing in Sanchi, Gwalior, and Agra,[34] Forster describes the
images rushing by his window. From this one can see his remarkable ability to evoke the texture of his Indian experiences:

> The Egyptian East has been Royal Academised, but not the In-
> dian. Sometimes everything was strange, like the final riot of glory
> at Tundla Junction, sometimes a Surrey landscape of heath and
> blue distance would have buffaloes wallowing in a pond or scarlet
> lumps in the middle of a field. Dawn revealed people walking
> beautifully, and it is thcsc motions that strike me even more then
> their colours or clothes. Whether a man washed his legs or a child
> its whole body in the Railway station fountain, whether a porter
> carried two trunks and a hat box on his head or Baldeo [his new
> servant] strides with a sharp check of his body when his foot is at
> its full extent, I am struck by the individuality of their movements.
> No two bodies function alike.[35]

Forster's observations of the graceful physical qualities of Indians recur again and again in his diary, and he also celebrates
this classic human beauty in his novel, perhaps most memora-
bly in the account of Aziz's "victory banquet":

> when the Nawab Bahadur stretched out his hand for food or
> Nureddin applauded a song, something beautiful had been ac-
> complished which needed no development. This restfulness of ges-
> ture—it is the Peace that passeth Understanding, after all, it is the
> social equivalent of Yoga. When the whirring of action ceases, it
> becomes visible, and reveals a civilization which the West can dis-
> turb but will never acquire. The hand stretches out for ever, the
> lifted knee has the eternity though not the sadness of the grave.[36]

Toward the Frontier: Lahore and Peshawar

After a brief stay in Delhi, Forster proceeded by train to Lahore in order to visit what had been the capital of the Mughal Empire under Shah Jehan in the seventeenth century.[37] His stay in Lahore was a hurried jumble of sightseeing and ill-arranged visits, and Forster's diary records his general disenchantment with the place: "Don't like Lahore. There are gardens and trees and broad roads, but all is unfinished and dreary, dissevered from home life and native. The distances are immense and one rattles about in ill-informed tongas."[38] He and Dickinson visited the museum made famous by Kipling's *Kim* (known locally as "the Wonder House") and were taken to a Christian college, where Dickinson gave a speech based on the mistaken supposition that the audience was Hindu. Needless to say, the reaction was polite but icy. More chaotic sightseeing followed—Lahore Fort and the great Badshahi mosque were dispatched in rapid succession, but a visit to Shahdara, the tomb of the Emperor Jehangir, proved calming at the end of the day:

> Shahdara after an early tea and enjoyed it more than anything inside Delhi, owing to its lovely setting. The approach over the bridge of boats and through palms; the entrance into the first court, once fitted up for pilgrims; the second court with its raised central tank; the tomb itself, the marble sarcophagus inlaid with cyclamen: they have the beauty of loneliness. The country as viewed from the minaret is flat, but well timbered and diversified with minor tombs: that of the Emperor's wife—or was it mistress?—is at the end of the enclosure. Walked over the railway bridge and heard Jackals.[39]

Forster's experience in Lahore is mirrored elsewhere in his journey: a hectic and uncomfortable day is suddenly made right by a moment of peaceful solitude, and the unpleasantness of the immediate past—whether silly Anglo-Indian club chatter or a disquieting misunderstanding about travel arrangements—is mercifully wiped away.

Forster's ultimate destination was not Lahore, but Peshawar, the town guarding the approach to the fabled Khyber Pass.
Peshawar was the home of the Pathans, rugged hill tribesmen
of Afghan origin famed for their prowess in war. The Pathans
were central figures in the iconography of Anglo-India, for Kipling and other writers had firmly established them as the foremost of the "martial races." The Pathans were idealized as "real
men," in contrast to the "decadent" and "effeminate" Bengalis,
who were castigated for their aping of English ways.[40] Forster's
visit to this frontier region had been prompted by Kenneth
Searight's invitation, and on November 7, the three Englishmen
traveled to Peshawar by train. In his diary, Forster takes note of
the passing scene:

> Journey to Peshawar . . . scenery dull till the Jhelum when a
> queer desert began. Waterless ravines—surely formed by water—
> had cut into the earth whose original surface remained in places,
> and in the sunset suggested human architecture. Searight, unrec-
> ognizably splendid, met us. . . .[41]

The visit to Peshawar offered Forster his only close contact
with military life in India: he and his companions stayed with
Searight's regiment, the Royal West Kents, and were fêted at a
large dinner party in the regimental mess. Both Dickinson and
Forster came away with fond memories of their visit to Peshawar—they found the young officers warm and outgoing, and
it seems that Forster was expressing his own feelings when he
described Aziz's attitude towards the military: "Aziz liked
soldiers—they either accepted you or swore at you, which was
preferable to the civilian's hauteur. . . ."[42] Forster encountered
this relaxed atmosphere when, owing to a minor muddle that
recalls Fielding's lost collar stud in the novel, he was late for a
dinner party given in honor of his visit:

> Evening, so pleasant, began disastrously for me. I lost my stud,
> was ten minutes late for dinner and it was guest night. I supposed
> they had gone on, but found the whole mess waiting. Real
> kindness of C.O. [Commanding Officer] made me feel no one
> minded, but it was long through dinner before I swallowed my
> vexation on S.'s [Searight's] account. Band—which had waited for

me to play Roast Beef of Old England—performed during evening, and they danced—S. far the best and inspiring them.[43]

Even Dickinson, an ardent pacifist, shed his customary reserve and fell in with the gaiety of the scene, making a favorable impression on a group of men with whom he had virtually nothing in common. This was one of only two occasions (the other was at Chhatarpur) when Dickinson seems to have been in any way at ease in India. Forster later described his friend's effect on the young subalterns:

> He was instantly beloved. The young officers were charming to him, and looked so fine in their gay jackets that militarism became permissible. They called him "The Don," and said "I say, will he put you in a book?" to one another. They made him swallow prairie oysters. They got rather drunk, in exquisite style, while Bob Trevelyan sported with them, and Dickinson and the C.O. sat apart, a couple of benign but contrasted uncles.[44]

Forster's lasting impression of the evening was positive, and the final comments in the diary indicate his pleasure at being accepted so naturally in a setting entirely alien to him:

> Once "in" with the military they take one to their bosom. No gradations between hauteur and intimacy, as is natural with unreflecting men. I imagine they are good specimens—all young and merry and some able. White pillared verandah and scarlet coats bounding: jolly outpost of Empire, which one realises on its edges as nowhere.[45]

The highlight of Forster's journey to the frontier was his visit to the Khyber Pass, a narrow defile through which for centuries invaders had swept down onto the plains of Hindustan. Though Forster was fascinated by these rough mountain tribes, his reaction to them marks one of the few instances where he expresses a feeling of distance, of estrangement:

> Khyber not stupendous, but it impresses to drive at a level out of the desert into hills. Khaki and blue sky. After the entrance, the road rises over chaos; then—having followed the curve of a hill—sinks to Ali Masjid. There the caravans began and we sat watching Central Asia pass and repass. . . . Both sorts of camels, donkeys with hens and babies tied on their backs and sometimes quarrel-

ing. Costumes not brilliant, but a sense of splendour through dirt. Fine fierce youths. Finest effect returning when processions streamed over the broken ground like a divided river. At Jamrud they were disarmed. —A wonderful sight, but from a world too remote and savage to seem real. I could not mix with them as with a show in lower India. They were of the stage.[46]

Forster was least attracted to the Pathans and other "martial races" that most Anglo-Indians so emphatically preferred, probably as a reaction against the violence of frontier existence, but also because he never got an opportunity to become more familiar with this way of life and the people who lived it. Almost invariably in his Indian journeys, Forster became fonder of Indians the better he got to know them—and it was this that distinguished him sharply from Anglo-Indians, most of whom echoed the sentiments of a young woman in Simla who told Forster, "I came out with no feeling against Indians, and now I can't bear them."[47]

Simla: The Summer Capital

When Forster arrived at Simla in November of 1912, he was visiting a place about which an elaborate mythology existed. This small town, clinging improbably to a ridge in the foothills of the Himalayas, was the seat of the Government of India during the hot weather, and, as such, had become in the British imagination the legendary abode of Viceroys and small functionaries, greying civil servants and handsome young subalterns, elderly dowagers and bored but beautiful young wives. All these were thrown together in a setting carefully contrived to imitate England in every possible detail. Cheery English flowers, a proper Anglican church, rows of shops with mock-Tudor facades, fancy dress balls, and tidy rustic summer homes were some of the features that made Simla seem tolerably like home to many Anglo-Indians. To be sure, the atmosphere was as rarified as the mountain air, but for many exiles it provided the only respite from a life of constant discomfort and loneliness.

The image of Simla which prevailed in most minds, however, was largely the creation of Rudyard Kipling, whose *Plain Tales from the Hills* and *Departmental Ditties* had given readers in England a lasting impression of the town as a rather immoral place in which gossip, petty adulteries, and excessive drinking were the chief amusements.[48] Indeed, so forcefully had Kipling drawn this aspect of Anglo-India that many English people had little idea where art ended and life began. Leonard Woolf, writing of his early days as a colonial administrator in Ceylon, expressed this confusion:

> The white people were also in many ways astonishingly like characters in a Kipling story. I could never make up my mind whether Kipling had moulded his characters accurately in the image of Anglo-Indian society, or whether we were moulding our characters accurately in the image of a Kipling story.[49]

Forster's stay in Simla proved to be an important part of his Indian education, for it helped to crystallize in his mind exactly what he found so disturbing about Anglo-Indian society. One of the clearest features of *A Passage to India* is the almost total isolation of the Anglo-Indians from the people they claim to know and understand, and it was this stubborn and deliberate insularity that Forster found so unpleasant at Simla. To him, "the real India" consisted above all of Indians—and there were precious few of these at Simla in 1912. There were, of course, various carefully selected "show Indians," but their presence was hardly noticeable. Forster's rejection of the petty society he found in Simla is expressed in an essay of his on Kipling's poetry:

> Second-rate Anglo-Indian society may be an amusing theme for the cynic, but it is not inspiring, and one soon forgets the jumble of girls and subs and rickshaws that gallivant through the pages of the *Departmental Ditties,* leaving an odour of stale whiskey behind them. These vulgar little phantoms are not India.[50]

Simla's Olympian atmosphere, of the gods enjoying their lei-
sure, aroused Forster's distaste and inspired his portrait in the
novel of Sir Gilbert, the Lieutenant-Governor whose enlightened
response to the Chandrapore incident is only possible because
he has been "exempted by a long career in the Secretariat from
personal contact with the peoples of India."[51]

Fortunately, there was a good deal more to Forster's Simla
visit than the unsatisfying social atmosphere. His hostess was
the prolific Anglo-Indian novelist, Sara J. Duncan:[52] she and
her husband took him on a short trek to Fagu, a popular viewpoint to the north of Simla where Forster got his only look at the
Himalayas:

> Vastness, not newness. The Himalayas, nameless except for
> Gangotri and Jamnutri, filled the northeast, between which were
> tangled hills: between which and me was a deep valley. Fagu on a
> promontory, over which the Thibetan road fell into confusion. The
> road full of mules and of Pathans with long black hair who were
> mending it.[53]

Walking in the hills was a pleasant diversion for Forster,
but the impression was faint in comparison to the one left by
a highly unusual wedding that he attended. A Muslim family
residing in Simla (one of a very few) had invited Forster's hosts
to the marriage of their daughter, and the visitor from England
readily consented to come along. What he saw was a "modern
wedding" which sought to synthesize Western rationalism and
traditional Muslim practices. Forster wrote a lengthy account of
the event in his diary: for him, it symbolized many of the cultural growing pains of India and offered the unhappy spectacle
of traditional values and customs supplanted merely for the sake
of novelty. His description is full of finely attuned perceptions
that indicate the remarkable rapidity with which Forster had
come to understand Indian social conventions (he had been in
India only one month). It is also suffused with a fine sense of
the comical absurdity inherent in such a haphazard mixture of
East and West:

> Mrs. Cotes Mr. Digby and myself just back from a Mahomm-
> medan wedding on rationalist lines. A dais in the garden on which

were a sofa, arm chair and table: other tables edged with torn
fringe stood on the lawn. We—mostly clerks, Indian Eurasian European, and shopkeepers—sat on chairs; the humbler guests on a
carpet. Purdah ladies watched from the gallery of the house behind. After long delay, during which a vase of flowers was put on
each table, the Moulvi took the armchair; he was in black embroi-
dered with gold. The bridegroom looked self-possessed and disso-
lute. The bride was not veiled. They sat on the sofa. Guests mur-
mured "This is totally contrary to the Islamic law." A long
argument followed between the Moulvi and the bridegroom's
brother, who at last rose, and said in English that the ceremony
would begin with verses from the Koran. Which were read. Then
that a local poet would recite about Conscience in Urdu.

"The sun illumines the world with light. Blessed be the sun
and moon and stars without whom our pupils, that seem like stars,
could not see. But there is another light, that of Conscience—" and
then the poetry flagged, and conscience became a garden where
the Bulbul of eloquence ever sang and the dew of oratory dropped
continually, and those who neglected her would "roll among
thorns."

Having made the pair man and wife, the Moulvi gave a short
address to the effect that it was not important how one was married, but how one behaved after marriages, and while he was
speaking we were handed warm tea. It was depressing, almost
heart rending, and the problem of India's future opened to me. For
at one end of the garden burst a gramophone—"I'd rather be busy
with my little Lizzy"—and at the other, on a terrace before the
house, about 20 orthodox Muslims had gathered for the evening
prayer. Facing the sun, which sets over Mecca here, they went
through their flexions, bowing down till they kissed the earth in
adoration to God, while the gramophone burred ahead, and by a
diabolic chance, reached the end of its song as they ended the
prayer. They rejoined the other guests without self consciousness.
But in them was the only beauty and dignity. The rest was hideous
and tentative, entering a valley whose further side is still invisible
to me. . . .[54]

Forster recreated this atmosphere in A Passage to India in his
description of the "Bridge Party." The awkwardness of that attempt to reconcile East and West is very similar to the wedding
at Simla, but in the novel the failure to achieve "connection" is
made more ominous by the kites that hover overhead and the
impartial sky that erects "echoing walls of civility."[55] The trans-

formation that Forster's Simla wedding has undergone between the author's life and his art represents a paradigm of his method: personal experience is recreated, but the meaning is intensified because it is superimposed against a background which dwarfs human aspirations, assigning them only a small place in the scheme of the universe.

Patna: A Vision of Chandrapore

One of the primary purposes of Forster's first Indian journey was to visit his friend Syed Ross Masood. The two had originally planned to travel together for a month or so, but this proved impossible because of Masood's work. With the exception of a few rushed days in Delhi in November 1912, they did not meet again until January 1913, when Forster and Dickinson arrived at Patna, a ramshackle city on the Ganges several hundred miles from Calcutta. Masood had established a law practice at Patna, and his fame as a recent Oxford graduate and the grandson of Sir Syed Ahmad Khan had brought him a large number of clients for a fledgling barrister.[56] Despite his success, Masood was unhappy: he complained about the constant corruption and lies with which he had to deal from day to day, and his disillusionment with his chosen career was heightened by a feeling that his talents and training were being wasted. Dickinson's diary contains a reference to some of the difficulties Masood faced:

> Masood found his opposing counsel signalling to a witness under cross examination whether to say yes or no. A client came to him, with his ear cut off, accusing a man of doing it. M. asked how many witnesses he had—"How many do you want?"[57]

Dickinson's diary is also the source of one of the most explicit connections between Masood and the character of Aziz in *A Passage to India*. Dickinson recalls Masood's state of mind in a description of an evening's conversation:

Masood and his grievances against the English, eg 1) an Englishman had ordered him to turn out of a railway carriage 2) has asked
him what the devil he meant by calling in English clothes 3)
rudely refused to receive him when he called—the Collector here
put a native in prison for bicycling in front of his carriage.[58]

Virtually all these incidents appear in the novel in some form or
another, utilized by Forster to illustrate Anglo-India's desperate
effort to maintain its lofty status in the face of a growing class of
educated Indians demanding social equality. Mrs. Turton's dismay at the sight of Indians driving into the club instead of
approaching on foot[59] and Ronny's mockery of an Indian in English clothes[60] lie close to the heart of Foster's contention that
manners are much more than "a side issue"[61] in the Raj. It was
from Masood that Forster gathered instances of rudeness to
Indians to give substance to his indictment of Anglo-India's
social values.

Forster's visit to Patna (or Bankipore, as the British section
of the city was called) was important because it suggested to
him the physical composition of Chandrapore, the town in his
novel. In the "Author's Notes" to the Everyman edition of A
Passage to India, Forster provided valuable clues to the origins
of both characters and locations in the book, and his first note
clearly indicates the relative importance of Patna in his creation
of the locale: "Chandrapore was suggested geographically by
Bankipore, but its inhabitants are imaginary."[62] Since Forster
met few Anglo-Indians in Patna (and these he rather liked), it
seems that the English of Chandrapore are an amalgam of unpleasant Anglo-Indians encountered in various towns during his
visits. But a comparison of the physical setting of the British
civil station of Bankipore with Forster's Chandrapore reveals a
close correspondence between the two.

Probably the best general description of Patna is the one
contained in the journals of Francis Buchanan-Hamilton, an extraordinarily energetic Englishman who conducted the first survey of Patna and Gaya districts in 1811–12, about a hundred
years before Forster's visit. Traveling by horse or on foot in what
was then one of the more remote areas of the Upper India

plains, Buchanan-Hamilton completed a detailed account of the region which even today has not been surpassed. His private journals of his travels are full of acute observations and minute descriptions: his comments on Patna give a clear picture of this sprawling and disheveled city that still retains its reputation as one of the least attractive places in India:

> There is one street tolerably wide that runs from the eastern to the western gate, but it is by no means straight nor regularly built. Every other passage is narrow, crooked, and irregular. The great street, when it breaks into sloughs, is occasionally repaired with earth thrown in by the convicts, the others are left to nature by the police, and the neighbors are too discordant to think of uniting to perform any work. Paving, cleaning, and lighting, considered so essential in every European town in such circumstances, are totally out of the question. In the heats of spring the dust is beyond credibility, and in the rains every place is covered with mud, through which however it is contrived to drag the little one-horse chaises of the natives. In the rainy season, there is in the town a considerable pond or lake, which, as it dries up, becomes exceedingly dirty, and in spring is offensive. . . . The inside of the town is disagreeable and disgusting, and the view of it from a distance is mean. Indeed, at a little distance south from the walls it is not discernible: there is no building that overtops the intervening trees, and no bustle to indicate the approach to a city. The view from the river, owing to the European houses scattered along its bank, is rather better, and is enlivened by a great number of fine-formed native women that frequent the banks to bring water. Still, however, the appearance of the town from thence, especially in the dry season, is very sorry, the predominant feature being an irregular high steep bank of clay without herbage, and covered with all manner of impurities, for it is a favorite retreat of the votaries of Cloacina, accompanied by the swine and curs that devour the offerings.[63]

Forster and Dickinson were less censorious in their comments about Patna, but the dreary and dusty qualities of the place figure prominently in their impressions. Dickinson's only remark on the city itself is a singularly laconic entry in his diary ("And Patna itself is only this street"),[64] but Forster retained a sharp image of the city in his mind which he reproduced as the opening of the novel he began writing shortly after returning from India in 1913. With the exception of one vital detail (the Barabar Hills, where the famous caves are located, are actually some fifty miles distant and are not visible from Patna), the description of Chandrapore is surprisingly similar to Buchanan-Hamilton's account of Patna:

> Except for the Marabar Caves—and they are twenty miles off—the city of Chandrapore presents nothing extraordinary. Edged rather than washed by the river Ganges, it trails for a couple of miles along the bank, scarcely distinguishable from the rubbish it deposits so freely. There are no bathing-steps on the river front, as the Ganges happens not to be holy here; indeed there is no river front, and bazaars shut out the wide and shifting panorama of the stream. The streets are mean, the temples ineffective, and though a few fine houses exist they are hidden away in gardens or down alleys whose filth deters all but the invited guest. Chandrapore was never large or beautiful, but two hundred years ago it lay on the road between Upper India, then imperial, and the sea, and the fine houses date from that period.[65]

In complete contrast to the "native" areas of Patna was the British civil station of Bankipore, which Forster got to know gradually and found far more pleasant. Built around a large oval maidan, Bankipore contained the solid houses of the British civil authorities, many of them surrounded by lush gardens and tropical trees; next to the maidan was an elongated, meandering hospital.[66] Forster's description of Chandrapore's civil station differs only slightly from this, though Bankipore is closer to the Ganges than its fictional counterpart:

> Inland, the prospect alters. There is an oval Maidan, and a long sallow hospital. Houses belonging to Eurasians stand on the high ground by the railway station. Beyond the railway—which runs parallel to the river—the land sinks, then rises again rather steeply. On this second rise is laid out the little civil station, and viewed hence Chandrapore appears to be a totally different place. It is a city of gardens. It is no city, but a forest sparsely scattered with huts. It is a tropical pleasaunce washed by a noble river. The toddy palms and neem trees and mangoes and pepul that were hidden behind the bazaars now become visible and in their turn hide the bazaars.[67]

Some elements of this description are taken from Forster's diary, which notes, "Mahmoud's roof—view over pepita toddy palm mango malaria-melon trees . . ."[68] and there is also a similar account of Bankipore in a letter Forster wrote to Bob Trevelyan, who by January of 1913 had moved on to South India and Ceylon:

> I wonder how you like South India. I must make the roofs of Bankipore do instead. There are so many Toddy Palms and malaria-melon trees that the views from them are quite tropical. (In case you puzzle over malaria-melon, it is a tree with fruit as big as melons which are good for malaria). Foul as the place is, there is enough going on to amuse one, and I have met several people, not all very nice. . . . Sometimes I bicycle, sometimes by the tide of Ganges do complain. I see steamboats on it but it is difficult to find when and where they go and whither.[69]

Forster's stay in Patna was quiet: a major event was the discovery of a krait (an extremely poisonous snake) in Masood's garden ("kerait in the garden, and it appears the servants have killed another and said nothing. Having strolled about in the dark or sockless we had a turn").[70] The usual sights were visited, the foremost being the Golghar, a bizarre structure resembling a beehive which the British had built as a granary in the eighteenth century. Another activity was visiting Masood's friends—and here Forster met some of India's foremost intellectuals, including Sachchidananda Sinha, editor of the influential *Hindustan Review,* and Syed Mahmoud, a well-known barrister who was one of the leading Muslim members of the Indian National Congress.[71]

The only Englishmen Forster seems to have met were two professors at Patna College, Charles Russell and V. H. Jackson, but they were probably instrumental in providing Forster with the background for one of the central settings in his novel. Both Russell and Jackson were busy studying early Buddhist inscriptions in the nearby Barabar Hills, and it is more than likely that it was their suggestion that Forster visit the caves there. Jackson was one of the founders in 1915 of the Bihar and Orissa Research Society, which concerned itself primarily with studying the many ancient sites in the area around Patna, and both men were later known for their discovery of new inscriptions in the Barabar Hills.[72]

The purpose of Forster's visit to Patna (Bankipore) was to see Masood again, and this provided ample diversion for him. But the brief entries in the diary indicate that the novelist's mind was constantly at work, giving shape and form to the random sights, sounds, and smells of the place, and storing them up for future use. It would, of course, be reductive to say that Chandrapore *is* Bankipore: all the characters and settings in Forster's novel are first and foremost imaginative ones, and it is misleading to suggest otherwise. Yet the powerful resemblances between the two towns are unmistakable, and the line between art and life is blurred. All the basic features of Bankipore—the dusty bazarrs and dark alleyways by the Ganges, the oval maidan surrounded by European houses, the long low hospital, the scattered palm trees trailing off into the dry, flat plain—figure prominently in the geography of Chandrapore.

Delhi and Aligarh: The Muslim Intelligentsia

One of the most persistent criticisms of *A Passage to India* concerns Forster's choice of a Muslim as the principal Indian character. Critics in both India and the West have accused Forster of sharing the Anglo-Indian prejudice that Muslims are somehow closer to European culture and its value system. One example of this instinctual preference for Muslims is a statement by John Morley, who was Secretary of State for India from 1906 to 1910. Morley was considered one of the more liberal and pro-Indian British officials, yet he too expressed a feeling of distance from Hindus, finding the basis for an understanding only in the Muslim community: ". . . I think I like Indian Mohammedans, but I can not go much further in an easterly direction."[73] This sense of a vague affinity between Muslim India and Christian England originated in a perception of Indian Muslims as inheritors of the proud traditions of the Mughal Empire, and therefore possessors of the familiar English values of "activity, masculinity, and forcefulness." [74] Another factor was, of course, the analogy between one mighty empire and another, a connection which gave the English a further boost in self-esteem.

The sharpest criticism of Forster's novel on this point has come from the well-known Indian writer Nirad C. Chaudhuri, who argues that Forster is wrong in choosing Aziz as his Indian protagonist because the Muslims were simply a sideshow in the struggle for Indian independence. He attacks the novel further on the grounds that Aziz and the other Indian characters "belong to the servile section and are all inverted toadies." [75] In Chaudhuri's view, those who fought for independence under the Congress banner are the only Indians worthy of serving as protagonists in a novel about the Raj, while all others are "toadies" whom he scorns. A strong element of condescension can be detected in Chaudhuri's attitude towards Aziz, whom he characterizes as a lower form of life: "Aziz would not have been allowed to cross my threshold, not to speak of being taken as an equal." [76] Forster himself sensed the snobbery implicit in Chaudhuri's criticism when the two men met in later years; his reaction to Chaudhuri was bemused, but he was shrewd enough to detect the aristocratic undertone and all that it implied: "He announced with some firmness that Aziz would never have been admitted into his ancestral home. This does not matter for Aziz, who has after all elsewhere to go, but it made me wonder whether I should have been admitted either." [77]

The important point here is that Forster was in no way attempting in *A Passage to India* to present a systematic picture of India and its people: Aziz and the other Indian characters are recognizable above all as human beings and not as stock figures representing "Hindu India," "Muslim India," or any other India. When questioned about this in 1962, Forster replied that the characters in the novel, although based on specific friends from his Indian days, are neither caricatures nor representations of one community or another:

> Q: It has been said that you understand your Muslim better than your Hindu. Aziz and Godbole come to mind. Would you comment?
> A: Some of my best friends have been Muslim. I have been attracted by Islamic culture, but I do not like the orderliness of Islam. In any case I have not thought much about religions. . . . Aziz is modeled on Masood, my greatest Indian friend. To him I dedicated *A Passage to India*. Godbole is also modeled on a friend. But I think of them—of Aziz and Godbole—as people and not as religious types.[78]

Forster's attitude toward Islam is a mixed one: although attracted by the sense of calm which is expressed in the simplicity of Islamic design and architecture, he was at the same time repelled by what he saw as its sternness and rigid moral sense. His feelings about Hinduism are similarly divided—the spirit of affirmation and gaiety in Hinduism moved him, but he found the trappings of Hindu ritual aesthetically unappealing. Actually, his interest in both religions was motivated by personal rather than aesthetic or philosophical considerations. Affection for his friends led Forster to consider their ways of viewing existence, some of which he incorporated into his own outlook. The Muslims in his novel, with the exception of Aziz, are not based upon any specific acquaintances, but are derived from prolonged contact with a talented and dynamic group of Indian Muslims whom Forster met on his first visit to India. Men like Hamidullah and the Nawab Bahadur are not "toadies," as Chaudhuri would have it: they are intelligent and perceptive men keenly aware of their delicate position in India as a distinct minority in an uncertain period of social and political change. The same is true of Forster's Muslim friends, men like the Ali brothers, Mohammed and Shaukat Ali, and Dr. M. A. Ansari, who later served as president of both the Muslim League and the Indian National Congress. It is to them we must turn to understand the curiously equivocal nature of the Muslims in the novel.

The Muslims Forster knew were men of considerable achievement: most were from middle-class backgrounds and, having excelled early in their studies, went on to the Muhammadan Anglo-Oriental College at Aligarh and then to England. When Forster arrived at Delhi in November 1912, he found a dedicated coterie of men deeply involved in public affairs. His entrée into this world came through Syed Ross Masood, who had rushed up to Delhi from Patna to spend a few days with his newly arrived friend. Taking Forster in hand, Masood showed him around Delhi and introduced him to numerous acquaintances.

One of the first Indian friends Forster made on his Delhi visit was the famous Muslim activist Mohammed Ali, who in 1912 was in his mid-thirties. Educated at Aligarh and Oxford, Mohammed Ali had taken the entrance examination for the Indian Civil Service but failed. He had then served in the government of the Hindu state of Baroda in western India, but had left that post in 1911 and gone to Calcutta, where he started a progressive Muslim newspaper called *Comrade*. This venture was a great success, and when the British shifted the capital from Calcutta to Delhi later that year, Mohammed Ali brought *Comrade* to Delhi in order to be near the center of power. The first Delhi issue of *Comrade* appeared in October 1912, only a few weeks before Forster's arrival.[79]

Forster met Mohammed Ali and his associates at a moment when the Balkan War was at its height, and much of the Indian Muslim community was in a state of near-hysteria over the severe defeats inflicted on the Turks by an alliance consisting of Serbia, Bulgaria, Montenegro, and Greece. Turkey was viewed by Indian Muslims as the last stronghold of Islamic rule: its sudden and unexpected military reverses at the hands of a hastily assembled coalition of weaker states was seen as a disaster for all the Islamic world. Forster's diary records the emotionally charged atmosphere among his friends at the time:

> We looked into the Comrade offices, and there was Mohammed Ali who exclaimed "I am absolutely miserable. The Bulgarian Army is within 25 miles of Constantinople." Nearly crying, he went with

Masood into another room: "Let no quarter be asked and none
given now. —This is the end." I am sure he was moved. . . . M.
[Masood] said "This is the turning point of my career . . . we shall
give to the Turks all the money that we have collected for the new
University."[80]

Forster viewed this melodramatic response as typical of the
Muslim community in times of stress, and it may well be that
Aziz's histrionic behavior before his trial and his frequent out-
bursts of poetic lamentation at the sad state of Indian Islam
were derived from Forster's experience of these activists in 1912
and 1913.[81]

Another of Forster's close friends was Dr. M. A. Ansari, an
extremely important figure in both politics and medicine at the
time. Ansari was one of the most brilliant Indian physicians,
trained first in India and then in London. As a young man of
twenty-five, he topped the list of successful candidates for the
M.D. degree in 1905 and was appointed Registrar of Lock Hospital in London; later he served as House Surgeon at Charing
Cross Hospital, which acknowledged his outstanding contribu-
tions in surgery by opening a ward called the "Ansari Ward." In
London Ansari met Motilal Nehru and his son Jawaharlal; when
the three returned to India, Ansari became the Nehru family's
personal physician, a post he held until his death in 1936.
Through the Nehrus, Ansari became active in the independence movement, serving as a link between the Muslim League
and the Congress. He was held in such high regard by both
Hindus and Muslims that he served as president of both organi-
zations, presiding over the League in 1918 and 1920, and over
Congress in 1927. He was an intimate of Gandhi, and his beautiful Delhi home, "Dar-es-salaam" (the Abode of Peace), often
served as the Mahatma's headquarters whenever he visited
Delhi.[82]

Ansari arranged for Forster to view a *nautch*, an entertainment of elaborate dances popular in wealthy and cultured Muslim circles. Forster was pleased with the invitation ("Food at
8.0. Then off to the Nautch that Ansari would give me; he's as
kind as charming and I think as good as either."),[83] since it of-

fered him a look at Indian social life not normally accessible to most Englishmen. Major Callendar's exasperation with Aziz at the beginning of *A Passage to India* stems from his utter ignorance of the changes being wrought in Indian society ("He never realized that the educated Indians visited one another constantly and were weaving, however painfully, a new social fabric.").[84] This same blindness to change explains Ronny Heaslop's extraordinarily rude entry into Fielding's garden party later in the novel.[85]

Forster's meticulously detailed description of the evening's entertainment reveals the sheer delight he felt at seeing an aspect of India rarely offered to Western visitors. He was clearly flattered to be a guest in an Indian Muslim home and recorded every nuance of the experience in his diary:

> The Nautch was in a friend's house . . . it was a beautiful house. An arch in the wall; long white washed staircase; then terrace with flowers. The ladies had already arrived and salaamed us—one with a weak but very charming face and very charming manners: I was never tired of looking at her. The other was young and fat with a ring through her nose indicating virginity. This made her arrogant, they said, and she didn't attract me. Both were short. One could easily "lapse" into an oriental: I found myself discussing their points dispassionately. A long wait. Other guests—2 sorts of Hindus, a Parsi, finally Ansari. Another wait while the dancers robed, another while the instruments tuned, a third while she stood acquiring inspiration. The "Peacock" followed, culminating with a shawl or ribband of gold that she held between outstretched hands, quivering. Songs:—voice exercises, an address in the classical style to God; afterwards what we asked for. Left hand against face, right stretched out; emotion came to me through the harsh voice and music, so that I enjoyed myself. The drum would thunder in on the last note: this excited us. Though its function is only to beat time, and when the singer sank down in our midst, with her scarlet and golden robes spread round us, and sang love-songs, I realised what a Nautch must be to Indians. She danced . . . a little with the other girl, who had put on blue and green over her white knickerbockers, but her I did not like, nor did the others. All that had had [sic] in the first grew worse. Our heads were battered by her screams, we lay half asleep on the floor. I did not understand that it would go on till I went.

Ansari tried to make me kiss the singers, but I got off with a handshake from the premiere. I felt fond of her. Starlit terrace. Masood and Ansari saw me to the 1.0 train, and Delhi ended happily.[86]

One aspect of this experience that stayed with Forster and was expressed in his novel is the Muslim attitude toward art—in this instance dance, poetry, and music. Forster noticed the scorn that most Anglo-Indians had for any sort of art and detested this philistinism with all his heart. His comments on the state of the arts in Chandrapore are tinged with sarcasm:

> Their ignorance of the Arts was notable, and they lost no opportunity of proclaiming it to one another; it was the Public School attitude, flourishing more vigorously than it can yet hope to do in England. If Indians were shop, the Arts were bad form, and Ronny had repressed his mother when she inquired after his viola; a viola was almost a demerit, and certainly not the sort of instrument one mentioned in public.[87]

This attitude is contrasted with that of the small gathering of men at Aziz's bedside when he is ill: only Hamidullah and Aziz himself are formally educated, yet there is an instinctive appreciation of beauty in this Indian setting:

> Of the company, only Hamidullah had any comprehension of poetry. The minds of the others were inferior and rough. Yet they listened with pleasure, because literature had not been divorced from their civilization. The police inspector, for instance, did not feel that Aziz had degraded himself by reciting, nor break into the cheery guffaw with which an Englishman averts the infection of beauty. He just sat with his mind empty, and when his thoughts, which were mostly ignoble, flowed back into it they had a pleasant freshness. The poem had done no "good" to anyone, but it was a passing reminder, a breath from the divine lips of beauty, a nightingale between two worlds of dust.[88]

Forster's visit to Aligarh acquainted him with another segment of India's Muslim elite. He spent nearly a week visiting the Muhammadan Anglo-Oriental College founded by Masood's grandfather, and in the course of his stay there, met the principal members of the college faculty. In 1912, Aligarh was

sharply divided between traditionalists who wanted the college
to remain a center for conservative Islamic social values and
religious training, and the modernists (a circle to which Masood
and his friends belonged), who wanted Aligarh to function as a
nursery for future political leaders of India's Muslims. A further
issue at the time was the role of the college's English teaching
staff, a talented group of men (mostly Cambridge educated)[89]
who had served the institution since its inception but now
found themselves the center of a controversy because of demands that the Indian staff be given more power. It is characteristic of Forster that he came away from Aligarh without passing judgment, even in the privacy of his own diary, on this
quarrel or on the individuals involved. He enjoyed his contact
with all the contending parties and managed, as often in his Indian travels, to learn something from each new experience.

Forster's diary notes his impressions:

> The College—spreading over the plain like red mushrooms. No
> order and little beauty. The best court disfigured by kiosks of
> W. C.'s. Distances are enormous, and not bridged by telephone. It
> can take an entire morning to get information. The students, who
> are dressed in white duck, frock coat and fez, are of all types, but
> one that is thin, dirty, and bearded predominates. I was not at-
> tracted by them, but their teachers were decent.[90]

He found the social atmosphere rather pleasant, commenting
after a breakfast with some of the teachers, "Civility every-
where. Much enjoyed myself and was never conscious whether
it was an Indian or an Englishman I was talking to."[91] But at
other times the deepening fissures between Indians and Englishmen, often reflecting the growing divisions in the society
as a whole, were all too apparent to Forster:

> In fact life at Aligarh showed many seams. The English staff com-
> plained that they were not trusted to give the help they had hoped
> to give, but would be turned adrift as soon as the Mahommedans
> could stand without them: they could make some way with the
> students—not much, owing to the influence of The Comrade, a
> forward-Islamic paper "which told lies"—and none at all with the
> governing body. The Mahommedans had an air of desperation
> which may be habitual, but was impressive. . . .[92]

Toward the end of his stay in Aligarh, Forster went on a predawn excursion into the countryside, which exuded the same air of vague mystery and shapelessness that characterizes Aziz's excursion to the caves with Adela Quested and Mrs. Moore:

> False dawn—the sun's rays on the upper layers of air—came as we entered Aligarh city, and true dawn behind the great mosque. Then India which baffles description because there is nothing to describe—the cultivated earth extending forever. Mustafa, an ugly athlete of a boy, saw Green Pigeons, and they shot 7. They were pleased, but even in India there is no criterion among sportsmen, and while some say G. P.'s are rare and worth getting, others say they are common and laugh.[93]

This is the India which Forster recreates so vividly in *A Passage to India,* a land in which the sun fails to appear at the appropriate moment and where consistent standards cannot be expected. This "failure of the appropriate," exemplified by Godbole's appeals to Krishna ("Come, come") and by Adela's enthusiastic preface to the sunrise which refuses to appear on cue, frustrates the tidy notions of Anglo-India. Forster, however, accepts it as an illustration of the impermanence of worldly things and of "the imbecility of human intellect"[94] in these matters.

chapter 3

First Passage:
Princely India, 1912–13

Chhatarpur: An Intimate Visit

Forster's introduction to the world of princely India oc-
curred at Chhatarpur, a small native state nestled among the
rugged ravines of central India. Carrying an introduction from
Sir Theodore Morison (who had been private tutor to the Maharajah some years ago), Forster, Dickinson, and Trevelyan arrived at Chhatarpur in late November of 1912 to find themselves in a very different India from the one they had seen thus
far. The British Raj had had relatively little impact here: most of
India's so-called "native states" had few ties to the modern
world, and their rulers, who had sworn fealty to the British
crown in a modern parody of feudal vassalage, were autocrats
with virtually unlimited powers. Some of the larger states like
Baroda, Mysore, and Hyderabad had adopted modern methods
of administration and education, but most others clung tena-
ciously to traditions of autocratic rule that stretched back, in
some cases, to medieval India. By Forster's time, however, the
realities of imperial politics had intruded upon even the most
isolated princely states, and the numerous rajahs and maharajahs found themselves obliged for the first time to heed inclina-
tions other than their own. In the year 1912, then, many of the
Indian princes were in a confused and uncertain frame of mind.
Within their own states, they still possessed absolute powers in
theory, but often had to defer to the wishes of the local Political
Agent (or Resident) who served as the representative of the Raj.[1]
This anomalous state of affairs had led to some testing of the
British resolve: many of the highly publicized excesses of cer-

tain maharajahs around the turn of the century can be traced to a stubborn determination to reassert their sovereignty in the face of an obviously more powerful state.

The princes of India came to be regarded in the Western world as embodiments of oriental splendor and lavish opulence, as "ornaments of Empire." Thrust into the giddy limelight of fashionable European society, the princes were more important as symbols than as real people: "Their gorgeous figures were a focal point at royal occasions like jubilees and coronations. And thus they learned the rich pleasures of the London season, the delectable savor of a Parisienne's laughter in the suave luxury of the Hotel Bristol and the gentle austerities of Marienbad. They became an indispensible part, like orchids and champagne, of the Edwardian age."[2] Side by side with this image of the maharajahs at play in Europe went the popular notion of their Indian domains that was expressed by Kipling, who called the native states "the dark places of the earth, full of unimaginable cruelty, touching the Railway and the Telgraph on one side, and, on the other, the days of Harun-al-Raschid."[3]

The Maharajah of Chhatarpur,[4] however, was neither an Edwardian dandy nor an odious oriental despot: he was, in Forster's words, "a tiny and fantastic figure, incompetent, *rusé*, exasperating, endearing."[5] In an interview given in 1962, Forster stated that the character of Godbole in *A Passage to India* was "modeled on a friend."[6] Although most critics have assumed that the friend in question is the Rajah of Dewas, it now seems clear that Forster had in mind the ruler of Chhatarpur, who was his host in 1912 and again, more briefly, in 1921. Forster utilized numerous details of the Maharajah's appearance and personality to create the enigmatic Brahman of his novel. From his dress, an odd mixture of East and West, to his insistent longings for union with the divine, the Maharajah of Chhatarpur is recreated in the figure of Godbole. Forster's account of Godbole, who first appears at Fielding's tea party, is rich in visual detail:

> He was elderly and wizen with a grey moustache and grey-blue eyes, and his complexion was as fair as a European's. He wore a turban that looked like pale purple macaroni, coat, waistcoat,

dhoti, socks with clocks. The clocks matched the turban, and his whole appearance suggested harmony—as if he had reconciled the products of East and West, mental as well as physical, and could never be discomposed.[7]

A description of the Maharajah of Chhatarpur that echoes the passage above comes from a letter written to Forster by J. R. Ackerley, whom Forster had recommended for a temporary post as Private Secretary to the Maharajah. Writing in 1923, Ackerley describes the aging ruler more than ten years after Forster first met him:

> He was clad in a round green velvet hat, thickly embroidered with gold; a kind of drab mauve tweed frock-coat with velveteen cuffs and collar of elephant grey, white linen trousers, purple socks of a vivid hue, and dancing pumps. He is now a sufferer from rheumatism (a favourite topic of conversation) and walks *péniblement,* his feet pointing one East, one West, like a decrepit man.[8]

A central connection between Godbole and the Maharajah of Chhatarpur is the religious and philosophical impulses that motivate them: in one of the most crucial scenes in the novel, Godbole sings a religious song for the guests assembled in Fielding's garden, and then goes on to illuminate its meaning:

> "I will explain in detail. It was a religious song. I placed myself in the position of a milkmaiden. I say to Shri Krishna, 'Come! come to me only.' The god refuses to come. I grow humble and say: 'Do not come to me only. Multiply yourself into a hundred Krishnas, and let one go to each of my hundred companions, but one, O Lord of the Universe, come to me.' He refuses to come. This is repeated several times. The song is composed in a raga appropriate to the present hour, which is the evening."
> "But he comes in some other song, I hope?" said Mrs. Moore gently.
> "Oh, no, he refuses to come," repeated Godbole, perhaps not understanding her question. "I say to him, Come, come, come, come, come, come. He neglects to come."[9]

Since this explanation ends with an appeal that is not answered, it can only mystify the English visitors. Their religion is based on an orderly system of cause and effect in which it is assumed that the worshipper's "curt series of demands on Jehovah"[10] will always be carefully acknowledged by the deity. Forster sees Godbole's metaphysical longing for the god Krishna as an essential aspect of Hinduism's dogged pursuit of otherworldly values, and the final section of the novel presents the festival celebrating the birth of Krishna as a joyously affirmative expression of this seeking after the divine. Forster recounts in his diary a conversation in which the Maharajah discussed his religious beliefs:

> In a courtyard at Rajgarh: "Do you meditate?" H. H. [His Highness]: "Yes—when I can, for 2 hours, and when I am busy for 45 minutes."—"And can you concentrate and forget your troubles?"— "Oh no, not at all; they come in with me—always—unless I can meditate on love, for love is the only power that can keep thought out. I try to meditate on Krishna. I do not know that he is a God, but I love Love and Beauty and Wisdom, and I find them in his history. I worship and adore him as a man. If he is divine he will notice me for it and reward me, if he is not, I shall become grass and dust like the others." [11]

The Maharajah's familiarity with Western philosophy at times adds a different tone to his conversation, but the impulses of his religious life are the same as Godbole's. In his early diary entries, Forster does not emphasize the mystical aspects of the Maharajah's seeking, but the second visit to India provided him a better glimpse of the Hindu mystical tradition at Dewas and he added this element to the character of Godbole in the later chapters of the novel. In any case, much of the time Forster and Dickinson spent at Chhatarpur was taken up in extensive religious and philosophical discussions with the ruler, who had an insatiable appetite for these talks in which Eastern and Western thought were freely mixed. Forster remembers the Maharajah's plaintive questioning of Dickinson: 'Tell me, Mr. Dickinson, where is God? Can Herbert Spencer lead me to him, or should I prefer George Henry Lewes? Oh, when will Krishna come and be my friend? Oh, Mr. Dickinson!" [12] Dickinson, who liked very little about India, was moved by the fervent sincerity of the Maharajah, and between these two unlikely friends there sprang up, as Forster calls it, "an instant sympathy." [13] They went for drives together in the Maharajah's car: Dickinson recalls "the long trains of bullocks leaping wildly into the ditch as he passed, absorbed in questions about Plato or Herbert Spencer."[14] In a letter home, Dickinson describes one of these drives, during which he detected in the drift of the conversation another motive for the Maharajah's longing for Krishna, a personal one more readily comprehensible to Western minds—loneliness:

> The Maharajah motored me this afternoon to a ruined palace on the lake—the most beautiful and appealing place I have ever seen. The lake is grown over with lotus leaves; there are water-fowls, and great trees hanging over the water and the usual wonderful sunset light. Sun too hot even at four. The Maharajah offered me the ruined palace (he offered it to Forster before) if I would come and live here. Shall I? I should sit in marble halls and courts and paddle on the lake. And close by is the lovely tomb of the Queen who was a nymph and lived on lotus and was called the daughter of the lotus. This is the Maharajah's account of her. Mosquitoes are getting tiresome and will shortly drive me under my curtains. . . . Púm Púm Púm—Tú Tu Tu Tu Tú Tu Tu Tu Tu Tá, says the drum. It's a queer world. As we emerged from the palace, the car stopped and the Maharajah held a long colloquy with an old woman with a child in her arms. "It's my cook," he told me, "She's always running away here to her home, and she says she won't come back this time." "Why not?" "She says her wages are too small. She gets two rupees a month and she wants four." The ordinary wage for an agricultural labourer is ld a day. "Perhaps that is why Krishna does not come." In explanation of this last I should say that the Maharajah's *sehnsucht*—touching and sympathetic to me—was always for Krishna to come—the ideal friend. As to the cook, he added that the principal reason why he missed her was that, when he couldn't sleep, he sent for her to talk philosophy and religion with him. That, at least, is democratic in a way inconceivable anywhere in the West.[15]

This longing for both human and divine companionship was a powerful impulse in the Maharajah, as Forster's friend Joe Ackerley immediately divined in 1923:

> He wanted some one to love him—His Highness, I mean; that was his real need, I think. He alleged other reasons, of course—an English private secretary, a tutor for his son; for he wasn't really a bit like the Roman Emperors, and had to make excuses.
> As a matter of fact, he had a private secretary already, though

an Indian one, and his son was only two years old; but no doubt he felt that the British Raj, in the person of the PA [Political Agent] who kept an eye on the State expenditure and other things, would prefer a label—any of the tidy buff labels that the official mind is trained to recognise and understand—to being told, "I want some one to love me." But that, I believe, was his real reason nevertheless.[16]

One can see, then, why Forster found the Maharajah of Chhatarpur memorable: his beliefs were a fascinating jumble of Western rationalism and traditional Hindu religiosity, and the man himself was affectionate and not afraid to express his emotions. In creating the character of Godbole, Forster has taken the Maharajah as his principal model, divesting him of his Western traits and retaining only the core of the ruler's character—his search for union with the divine as a means of attaining universal love.

While at Chhatarpur Forster and Dickinson were privileged to witness several religious plays consisting of scenes from Krishna's boyhood. These performances, which Forster likened to medieval mystery plays and Dickinson to early Greek drama, were danced by young male actors from the Maharajah's court. Dickinson has written the most vivid account of these plays in his *Appearances*. He explains their meaning, registering profound admiration for this new but strangely appealing art form:

A few lamps set on the floor lit up the white roof. On either side the great hall was open to the night; and now and again a bird flew across, or a silent figure flitted from dark to dark. On a low platform sat the dancers, gorgeously robed. All were boys. The leader, a peacock-fan flashing in his head-dress, personated Krishna. Beside him sat Radha, his wife. The rest were milkmaids of the legend. They sat like statues, and none of them moved at our entry. But the musicians, who were seated on the ground, rose and salaamed, and instantly began to play. . . . Suddenly, as though they could resist no longer, the dancers, who had not moved, leapt from the platform and began their dance. It was symbolical; Krishna was its centre, and the rest were wooing him. Desire and its frustration and fulfillment were the theme. Yet it was not sensual, or not merely so. The Hindus interpret in a religious spirit this legendary sport of Krishna with the milkmaids. It symbolises the soul's wooing of God. And so these boys interpreted it. Their passion, though it included the flesh, was not of the flesh. The mood was rapturous, but not abandoned; ecstatic, but not orgiastic. There were movements of a hushed suspense when hardly a muscle moved; only the arms undulated and the feet and hands vibrated. Then a break into swift whirling, on the toes or on the knees, into leaping and stamping, swift flight and pursuit. A pause again; a slow march; a rush with twinkling feet; and always, on those young faces, even in the moment of most excitement, a look of solemn rapture, as though they were carried out of themselves into the divine. . . . For the first time I seemed to catch a glimpse of what the tragic dance of the Greeks might have been like. The rhythms were not unlike those of Greek choruses, the motions corresponded strictly to the rhythms, and all was attuned to a high religious mood. In such dancing the flesh becomes spirit, the body a transparent emblem of the soul.[17]

Forster's account of the same play is much briefer, but it also takes note of the passionate ecstasy of this devotional dance which glorifies the body without sensuality and thus makes it an "emblem of the soul":

Krishna and Radha wore black and gold. What to describe—their motions or my emotions? Love in which there neither was nor desired to be sensuality, though it was excited at the crisis and reached ecstacy. From their quieter dancing, dignity and peace. The motions are vulgarised by words—little steps, revolutions, bounds, knee-dancing—how clumsy it gets and will my memory always breathe life into it? Radha was most beautiful and animated, but a little touched by modernity; and Krishna, hieratic, his face unmoved while his body whirled, soared highest.[18]

The elderly Rajah of Mau in *A Passage to India* also keeps a company of religious dancers—Forster's description in the novel is clearly taken from his experiences at Chhatarpur:

He [the Rajah] owned a consecrated troupe of men and boys, whose duty it was to dance various actions and meditations of his faith before him. Seated at his ease, he could witness the Three Steps by which the Saviour ascended the universe to the discomfiture of Indra, also the death of the dragon, the mountain that turned into an umbrella, and the saddhu who (with comic results) invoked the God before dining. All culminated in the dance of the milkmaidens before Krishna, and in the still greater dance of

Krishna before the milkmaidens, when the music and the musicians swirled through the dark robes of the actors into their tinsel
crowns, and all became one.[19]

At this point the resemblance ceases between the inhabitants of
Mau in the novel and those of Chhatarpur: Forster wrote that
the characters in his fictional native state are "imaginary, and
there is, in particular, no original for the aged Rajah."[20] Yet
clearly the Maharajah of Chhatarpur had charmed Forster and
his companions, offering them a glimpse of a subtle mind that
combined familiar Western notions with new and baffling Indian concepts of religious endeavor. Other English visitors also
stopped at Chhatarpur in the years before the Great War, but
not all were as favorable in their comments as Forster and Dickinson. Two noted British intellectuals who came to India ar-
dently seeking truths of a very different nature were the in-
trepid Fabian Socialists, Sidney and Beatrice Webb. In a letter
written to Forster in 1934, Beatrice Webb offered this scornful
picture of the Maharajah: "We also stayed with that 'tiny and
fantastic figure': we thought him the last word of Hindu deca-
dence and especially repulsive when he asked my husband to
help him to save his soul."[21] One can see even more clearly the
enormous gap between the Webbs' sensibility and that of Forster by looking at the end of this same letter, where Mrs. Webb
earnestly urges Forster to write another novel like A Passage to
India which will dramatize "the current conflict all over the
world between those who aim at exquisite relationships within
the closed circle of the 'elect' and those who aim at hygienic and
scientific improvement of the whole of the race."[22] This is distant indeed from the spirit of Forster's novel: it is not surprising
that the Webbs loathed Chhatarpur and the India it represented
in their minds. Forster, however, sympathized with the
Maharajah's searching for salvation—indeed, his first four
novels all explore in one way or another what it means to be
"saved"—and in any case he thought it wrong to condemn out
of hand the spiritual quests of others.

Chhatarpur provided another important element in the
making of A Passage to India, for its dramatic scenery stirred

him to take note of it in his diary on the first morning after his arrival:

> The view, which I feared the moonlight had romanticised, is beautiful always—thickly-wooded in front with the temples of the town in the foreground, and barer behind; while in every direction the graceful hills diversify it. The only idyllic place I have seen yet. The guest house is on a narrow ridge which rises to a temple of Hanuman. Bob and I went after breakfast, and a priest, like a cheerful Christ, skipped down the walls to greet us, dressed in a duster and smelling of ghee.[23]

Chhatarpur is located in one of the wildest and most inaccessible parts of the hills that cut across central India. The thick jungle terrain interspersed with small rivers houses a profusion of brilliantly colored vegetation and many animals. Forster describes an elephant ride which, though a bit frightening for such a recent arrival to India, was nevertheless delightful in the variety of new sights and sounds it revealed:

> Two miles along the Banda road, under a ridge where tigers live, then the Jungle. It was unlike what I had imagined, yet brought the expected feelings: powerful and hostile. The attendant handed up one fruit after another, all unripe and unknown, and as we advanced between brushwood and rocks, a slight reverberation—such as Reinhardt uses—came at intervals. P.S. [Private Secretary], like me, thought it a wild beast, but the Mahout said it was the elephant himself who made it when he thought the journey was ending. The Temple of the Goddess of Rain gleamed from a crag on the right. Round it the annual Fair is held every Friday when the rains come. We walked up. A tangle of boulders and trees with a little white-washed masonry: the goddess gesticulated inside, vermilion, but her Brahmin was away. The view was wild and beautiful. Descending we came to a marsh where the Elephant walked, picking rushes; in parts it was purple with some subaqueous growth, in others birds swam, and great trees grew by its edge.[24]

In his notes to the Everyman edition of *A Passage to India,* Forster gives a clear hint of Chhatarpur's importance in the creation of the third section of his novel: "The scenery and architecture of Mau were derived from two small Central Indian states, Chatterpore and Dewas."[25] Since Dewas is flat except for

the Hill of Devi in its center, the hilly terrain of Mau in the
novel must be that of Chhatarpur, and Forster has even borrowed from Chhatarpur the name of his fictional native state,
for the ruined summer palace of the Maharajah (the same place
to which Dickinson had been driven) was located at Mau, about
ten miles north of the town of Chhatarpur:

> Mau is on a lake, beyond which is a hill and tombs. One—200
> years old—is called the "Queen's." "She was a nymph and used to
> walk on the top of the water lilies." Here H. H. would meet
> Krishna, and is never happy on account of this loneliness. The Pal-
> ace is fine Hindu-Moslem work in the stucco that is so different
> from the English and can seldom be procured now. Hall, with col-
> umns down the centre, opens from its length on to a terrace, be-
> neath which is the Lake, reached by steps under a great tree. The
> water is full of growth, but clear. When the sun set ducks flew
> over and hundreds of teal beat the surface with their wings far
> away, making thunder.[26]

This setting is recreated almost exactly when Aziz goes riding to
the lake outside the town in the novel:

> The lane led quickly out of town on to high rocks and jungle. Here
> he drew rein and examined the great Mau tank, which lay exposed
> beneath him to its remotest curve. . . . He took the path by the
> sombre promontory that contained the royal tombs. Like the pal-
> ace, they were of snowy stucco, and gleamed by their internal
> light, but their radiance grew ghostly under approaching night.
> The promontory was covered with lofty trees, and the fruit-bats
> were unhooking from the boughs and making hissing sounds as
> they grazed the surface of the tank; hanging upside down all the
> day, they had grown thirsty. The signs of the contented Indian
> evening multiplied; frogs on all sides, cowdung burning eternally;
> a flock of belated hornbills overhead, looking like winged skeletons
> as they flapped across the gloaming. . . . The European Guest
> House stood two hundred feet above the water, on the crest of a
> rocky and wooded spur that jutted from the jungle.[27]

Aziz had come to Mau seeking an escape from the injustice and
tension of British India, and here Forster seems to have drawn
upon the peace he himself had found at Chhatarpur to realize
Aziz's sense of restfulness in his new home.

But even in this most quiet and calm portion of Forster's

Indian journey, he could not avoid the jarring presence of official Anglo-India, for very near to Chhatarpur lay Nowgong, the chief military cantonment for the Bundelkhand region. Largely made up of rugged uninhabited hills and ravines, this area was the natural haunt of armed bandits (*dacoits*) who preyed on Indians and English alike: even the august person of the Dewan (Prime Minister) of Chhatarpur was fair game.[28] Thus Nowgong took on in the late nineteenth century an exaggerated importance as the base for forays (usually unsuccessful) against the many marauders. In 1912, it was still an important station and, from an officer's point of view, an attractive one: the memoirs of those who served in Nowgong during their careers all give extravagant praise to the place for its hunting and shooting opportunities:

> Life in Nowgong was most enjoyable in these days. The station was not so large as to make life too strenuous or so small as to be dull. . . . The country of Bundelkhand is most attractive, with its series of low hills, lakes, forts, and small rajas' capitals dotted about it. The shooting was so excellent that in winter even moderate shots could go out in twos and threes and be sure of bagging fifty couple or so of snipe and a fair number of duck, teal and sandgrouse. Blackbuck, chinkara and pig were numerous, and black bear and panther not hard to come by.[29]

For someone who was not a gentleman officer, however, Nowgong could be dull—to Forster it was stultifying. Since the Maharajah of Chhatarpur was under the watchful eye of the Political Agent at Nowgong, Forster and Trevelyan (minus Dickinson, who was mercifully ill) were dutifully trundled off to the cantonment to pay their respects. The entry in Forster's diary seethes with annoyance at the place and its inhabitants: "Nowgong, a small cantonment and a bore; polo; officers' wives with hideous voices and faces of that even pink."[30] Among the predictable cast of characters was the army chaplain, a cheerful boor who shouted, "Come, Maharajah, why don't you eat beef? Do you good!" The attitude of the Indians toward this offensive man is indicative of the equanimity with which they had learned to greet insults. Forster records that he and Trevelyan

"winced with horror" at the remark, but were reassured pri-
vately by one of the Maharajah's advisers, who told them, "The
padre sahib is a very nice man indeed, he has no interest whatever in religion, and that is suitable for a clergyman."[31] Another
source of irritation was the Political Agent, who nearly undid
Forster's peace of mind with his narrow-minded talk:

> Tea with P.A. at Nowgong. Then we walked by a lake opposite
> Mau. He said—but I won't sully the beauty of the evening, which
> was very English, with orange sunset and black clouds. Then the
> peculiar purple that I've only seen in India appeared in its usual
> place—half-way up the western sky.[32]

Other official visits were required of Forster in Chhatarpur,
but these were a bit more pleasant and afforded him a look at
the workings of a small native state that was, like so many
others, minimally organized, with haphazard public services
and administration. An inspection of the local jail brought favorable comments in Forster's diary ("good health and the men
were gently making carpets and durries, or working in a garden
of sweet scents and fruits"),[33] and Chhatarpur State's *Annual
Report* for 1912 abruptly takes note, in the middle of a rambling
account of the accomplishments of the local hospitals, of a visit
by Forster and Trevelyan to Daly Hospital:

> Two hundred and thirty-six operations were performed during the
> year, all except one being reported as successful. Messrs. E. M.
> Forster and R. C. Trevelyan visited the hospital and made good
> remarks. In case [*sic*] of both the hospitals, European medicines
> are imported through the Agency Surgeon, while country ones are
> procured locally. About 312 goats were examined for slaughter and
> Bazar articles were also inspected at times.[34]

This recalls Aziz's casual medical practice at Mau, a random
mixture of Western and local remedies ("here in the backwoods
he let his instruments rust, ran his little hospital at half-steam,
and caused no undue alarm"):[35] Forster, always scrupulously
polite where anyone's feelings were involved, was more frank in
his diary, describing the hospital as "a muddled courtyard in
which the 'out' patients sat—very much 'out'."[36]

Chhatarpur itself, then, had given Forster a sharp mental

picture of a small princely state which remained with him ten years later when he was writing the final section of his novel, and the unusual Maharajah had shown him the workings of what Forster called "the Indian mind." Indian and Western modes of thinking are often presented in *A Passage to India* as mutually exclusive. Forster describes the bafflement of Aziz and his friends at Fielding's blunt words on his role in India:

> The Indians were bewildered. The line of thought was not alien to them, but the words were too definite and bleak. Unless a sentence paid a few compliments to Justice and Morality, its grammar wounded their ears and paralysed their minds. . . . They had numerous mental conventions, and when these were flouted they found it very difficult to function.[37]

Forster characterizes Indian thought as circuitous and elaborative, in contrast to the linear logic of the Western mind. In creating Professor Godbole, he drew upon his experiences at Dewas to give life to his account of the Brahman's religious devotions, but it was the Maharajah of Chhatarpur's bafflingly indirect personality that inspired Godbole's impenetrable demeanor. Forster may well have been thinking of the Maharajah when he gave this version of the difficult encounter between Indian and Western thought:

> The Indian who attempts to interpret his country to the Westerner is apt to become part of the mystery he offers to solve. He is too often full of vague platitudes, of illustrations that explain nothing, of arguments that lead nowhere, and such interpretation as he gives is unconscious. He leaves us with the sense of a mind infinitely remote from ours—a mind patriotic and sensitive—and it may be powerful, but with little idea of logic or facts; we retire baffled, and, indeed, exasperated.[38]

Dewas and Indore: Initial Visit

Forster's first stopover at the tiny state of Dewas Senior was as a tourist; although he came with English friends who were able to give him some explanation of this remarkable place, his stay of ten days offered only a superficial glimpse. In 1921, however, he returned for seven months as the private secretary to the Rajah of Dewas and this experience proved to be, in Forster's words, "the great opportunity of my life."[39] Very few Westerners in India are ever offered a chance such as Forster's to know Indians intimately and share their homes and lives. Forster's novel was profoundly influenced by Dewas because it became the part of India he knew best.

In 1912, however, Forster was only one of a large cheerful British party that had been invited by the Rajah of Dewas Senior to celebrate Christmas; his guide was Sir Malcolm Darling, whom he had known in England and who had first come to Dewas in 1907 as tutor to the young Rajah, then nineteen years old.[40] Darling and his exuberant young charge had become warm and affectionate friends. Although Darling was transferred after several years at Dewas to the Punjab (where he had a long and distinguished career in the civil service), he always came back to visit and proved a steady friend when the Rajah's later years became fraught with difficulties. The tie that bound Darling to Dewas was his affection for the young ruler, whom many different observers agreed was a most extraordinary personality.

Born in 1888, Tukoji Rao Puar III, Rajah of Dewas Senior, had acceeded to his title in 1900, but did not assume full powers until 1908.[41] He attended that famous "nursery of princes," the Mayo College at Ajmer, where he received his diploma "with distinction." Malcolm Darling arrived in Dewas in 1907 and soon took the young prince on an Indian version of the Grand Tour, a four months' journey through India, Burma, and Ceylon. Upon returning, the Rajah was married to Akkasaheb Maharaj, the favorite daughter of the Maharajah of Kolhapur, the premier Maratha prince in the Deccan because of his direct descent from the great hero Shivaji. A son and heir was born in 1911 (Vikramsinhji Rao Puar), and when Forster arrived in 1912 he found a thriving and happy household.[42] The Rajah of Dewas Senior had gained a reputation in official circles as a bright and progress-minded ruler who held great promise for the future:

> What the British officials must have liked most was his natural charm, his quick intelligence, his gaiety, his easy familiarity. He entertained them lavishly at elaborate champagne banquets; gave fancy dress balls for their entertainment and thoughtfully provided their costumes, too. He played an excellent game of tennis, was a wonderful host, a brilliant conversationalist, eager to do all the correct things, and he was full of plans for establishing political reforms in his state. Sir Valentine Chirol, the noted British journalist, a man certainly not given to unmerited praise, wrote of him as being "one of the most enlightened of the younger princes." [43]

It was for one of the Rajah's enormous entertainments that Forster and his English companions had come—there was to be feasting, music, and a procession, partially to celebrate Christmas but also to felicitate the recently married Goodalls, whom Forster knew from Bombay. The letters Forster sent home describing these gay and enjoyable days reveal an important aspect of his attitude toward India—he was eagerly responsive to new experiences, savoring each one for its own value and its broadening effect on his character, and he was always willing to adapt himself to Indian ways. An example of this is his delightful account of the elaborate Indian ceremonial clothes given to him for the festivities by the Rajah:

> Baldeo, much excited by the splendour that surrounded us, was making the best of my simple wardrobe and helping to snip my shirt cuffs where they were frayed, when there was a cry of "May I come in?" and enter the Rajah, bearing Indian raiment for me also. A Sirdar (courtier) came with him, a very charming boy, and they two aided Baldeo to undress and redress me. It was a very funny scene. At first nothing fitted, but the Rajah sent for other garments off people's backs until I was suited. Let me describe myself. Shoes—I had to take them off when the Palace was reached, so they don't count. My legs were clad in jodhpurs made of white muslin. Hanging outside these was the youthful Sirdar's white shirt, but it was concealed by a waistcoat the colours of a Neapolitan ice—red, white and green, and this was almost concealed by my chief garment—a magnificent coat of claret-coloured silk, trimmed with gold. I never found out to whom this belonged.

It came to below my knees and fitted around my wrists closely and very well, closely to my body. Cocked rakishly over one ear was a Maratha turban of scarlet and gold—not to be confused with the ordinary turban; it is a made-up affair, more like a cocked hat. Nor was this all. I carried in my left hand a scarf of orange-coloured silk with gold ends, and before the evening ended a mark like a loaf of bread was stamped on my forehead in crimson, meaning that I was of the sect of Shiva.[44]

The tone here is relaxed and easy despite the strangeness of the experience—most Anglo-Indians would likely have been uncomfortable in this situation, but Forster was charmed and flattered to be treated so warmly.[45]

That evening was Forster's first real Indian feast, spanning many hours and literally dozens of different dishes, all served in grandiose style on silver platters. The Indian mode of dining— everyone sits on the floor and eats with the right hand—was difficult to master, and the food itself hopelessly mysterious to Forster. A letter to his mother enumerates the various dishes at the banquet, and then goes on to describe his reaction to this vast meal:

> Some of the dishes had been cooked on the supposition that an elephant arrives punctually, and lay cooling on our trays when we joined them. Others were brought round hot by the servants who took a fistful and laid it down wherever there was room. Sometimes this was difficult, and the elder dishes had to be rearranged, and accomodate themselves. When my sweet rice arrived, a great pushing and squeezing took place, which I resented, not knowing how attached I should become to the newcomer. Everything had to be eaten with the hand, and with one hand—it is bad manners to use the left—and I was in terror of spoiling my borrowed plumes. Much fell, but mostly into the napkin, and the handkerchief I had brought with me. I also feared to kneel in the sauces or to trail my orange scarf in the ornamental chalk border, which came off at the slightest touch and actually did get onto the jodhpurs. The cramp, too, was now and then awful. The courtiers saw that I was in pain, and told the servants to move the tray that I might stretch, but I refused, nor would I touch the entire English dinner that was handed round during the meal—roast chicken, vegetables, blancmange, etc.[46]

In the interests of cultural purity, many Anglo-Indians shunned Indian customs and food. Anglo-Indian literature abounds with dire warnings about the dangers of "going native": [47] the slightest concession to Indian habits was considered a sign of potential moral decay. More often than not, it was the women who took up the cause of preserving the pristine "Englishness" of the Anglo-Indian community: in *Hindoo Holiday,* J. R. Ackerley writes of a confrontation with a stern arbiter of English values during his stay in Chhatarpur:

> This evening when I went up to the Guest House for dinner, Mrs. Bristow, the young wife of one of the Shikaripur officers, was sitting by the fire reading a book.
> "What are you chewing?" she asked, looking up at me.
> "A clove."
> "Well for heaven's sake don't! I can't bear the sight. I suppose you chew gum at home?"
> "No. I don't like chewing gum," I said.
> "Well, do spit that out."
> "But I like cloves."
> "Well, I don't. It's disgusting and irritating. Go on, spit it out!"
> "Certainly not."
> "Go on! I'm accustomed to being obeyed."
> "But obedience is a duty," I said; "and I have no duty towards you—except to see that you, too, are fed."
> For a moment she tried to fix on me the power of her eye (which works, I believe, upon the subalterns of her husband's regiment), but this also failed to move my clove.
> "Look here," she said, "let me give you a word of advice: don't go Indian!" [48]

Though spared such direct criticism, Foster was nevertheless acutely aware of the role he was expected to play. His delight at the carefully prepared Dewas feast, his willingness to make light of his own blunders, and his determination to do things as Indians would—all these point to a desire to experience India at first hand. Forster wanted to meet Indians on their own terms instead of on those dictated by condescending Anglo-Indians. His receptivity in these matters allowed him to enjoy himself fully and, more importantly, enabled him to develop close personal relationships with Indians which would otherwise have been impossible. The letter describing his festive evening in Dewas ends with a sentence which makes evident his already growing affection for the place and also indicates the qualities he found so appealing: "So ended a very charming evening, full of splendour yet free of formality." [49]

One of the most striking things about Dewas for Forster was the peculiar administrative arrangement, based upon a misunderstanding and perpetuated in the name of tradition. His own description of this is vivid and from it one can easily understand why Malcolm Darling once called Dewas "the oddest corner of the world outside Alice in Wonderland." [50]

> Unversed though I am in politics, I must really give you some account of this little state, which can have no parallel, except in a Gilbert and Sullivan opera. In the eighteenth century, the then Rajah, being fond of his brother, gave him a share in the government, and his descendants extended the courtesy to his (the brother's) descendants. When the English came (early nineteenth century) they seem to have mistaken the situation, and supposed that there were two independent rulers in the same city. They guaranteed both, with the result that now there are twin dynasties, with their possessions all peppered in and out of each other. Each has his own court, his own army, his own water works and tennis club, his own palace, before each of which different bands play different tunes at the same hour every evening.
>
> It is true that Devi—the sacred mountain that stands above the distracted city like an acropolis—has at least been divided between them, so that each can get to his own shrine without walking on the other's footpath; and it is true that they have come to an arrangement over the flagstaff at the top, by which it belongs to both of them—upper half to one, lower half to the other, and the flag at half-mast to be neutral. [51]

Forster soon began to wonder whether the entire experience was real or imaginary: "The arrangement must have been unique, and an authoritative English lady, who knew India inside out, once told me that it did not and could not exist, and left me with the feeling that I had never been there." [52] Dewas was teaching him a most important lesson about India—never to assume anything, never to conclude that reality could be defined by what one saw and understood rationally. In *The Hill of Devi,* Forster describes an incident (taken directly from his diary) which exemplifies this:

> . . . I walked up Devi before breakfast . . . and saw, down in the plain, a grave of earth under a peepul tree, polished roots forming its precincts. A garland of jasmine hung on the head of the grave, sticks of burning cotton wool soaked in incense were stuck in its sides, a heap of grain with divine cooking utensils lay in front. A man in a red turban told us that he was a clerk who wanted eight rupees per month instead of seven, and he came here to pray for this raise every Thursday. An old woman was there too: she kept the grave clean, for which a piece of land was settled on her. "A shrine of Durga," Malcolm thought, but he was wrong, it was Moslem; one was always going to be wrong.[53]

The very soil of Dewas exuded an atmosphere of vague uncertainty, and for the first time in his Indian travels, echoes of doubt and distrust creep into Forster's diary:

> Oh hostile soil. Stones and sudden little holes at dark. . . . A land of petty treacheries, of reptiles moving about too cautious to strike each other. No line between the insolent and the servile in social intercourse: so at least it seems to me.[54]

These discordant notes represent an abrupt shift in mood from the positive comments about the place and its people which characterize the diary entries on Dewas and Forster's letters home. But diaries may fail to convey significant undercurrents in the diarist's mind that are determining the tone: there is, after all, no real way of knowing what unspoken factors might have moved Forster to inject such an ominous note. It is a note slightly reminiscent of Mrs. Moore's sudden transformation in *A Passage to India* from an eager cultivator of human relationships to a sybil whose cryptic pronouncements augur some evil in the air. The brooding emotions stirred briefly in Forster at Dewas recurred only once more during his travels—on a visit to the extraordinary Barabar Caves.

About twenty miles south of Dewas on the great Bombay-Agra road lies the much larger city of Indore. The Indore ruling dynasty was founded by Malhar Rao Holkar during the great Maratha expansion of the eighteenth century, and by Forster's time, Indore was one of the most powerful Maratha states, surpassed only by Gwalior and Kolhapur. The Holkars were far more energetic rulers than the Puars of Dewas Senior, and by the mid-nineteenth century Indore had outstripped the older cities of the region (notably Dewas and Ujjain) to become an important commercial and political center.[55] Further prominence was given to Indore by virtue of the fact that the Agent to the Governor-General, or "Resident," for the vast Central India region lived there. A large area centered upon the Residency had been ceded to the British by the Holkars and served as an enclave for the official Anglo-Indian community. Sir Kenneth Fitze, the Resident at Indore for many years, describes this section of the city as it looked in the 1920s:

> It possessed in fact much of the charm and many of the familiar features of an English village. For the abode of the Squire there was a stately Residency with its pillard facade and stone balustrades glimpsed through parklike grounds from a *maidan*, which for present purposes I would translate as "village green," round which were spaced the abodes of the doctor, the chaplain and the various officials of the Agency. In one corner of the green the Residency Club nobly and convivially sustained the traditions of the English "local" and beyond it ran a lovely stretch of river which, with a wealth of water-lillies, two quaint stone bridges, and a little fleet of punts and canoes maintained by the Club, could challenge comparison with many a stream in Hampshire or Devon, though the illusion was apt to be marred by an exotic abundance of palm trees, apes, and peacocks. The Church with its square squat tower, the shady cemetery, the ultra-modern garage with its gleaming array of petrol pumps, and the modest emporium known as the "Central India Stores," were well in the English harmony, as also was the cottage hospital, devotedly staffed by Franciscan nuns.[56]

With the probable exception of the garage and petrol-pumps, this is very much the same Indore that Forster saw in 1912 and again in 1921, and the resemblances between Fitze's description and the account of Chandrapore in the novel cannot be ignored. Chandrapore is briefly described in the opening chapter:

"The civil station . . . is sensibly planned, with a red-brick club on its brow, and farther back a grocer's and a cemetery, and the bungalows are disposed along roads that intersect at right angles."[57] Although Forster stopped with Anglo-Indians every so often in 1912 and 1913, only in Indore did he have sustained contact with an insular, close-knit Anglo-Indian community similar to the one in Chandrapore. And only in Indore did he get a good look at that most durable of Anglo-Indian institutions, the club. According to his diary, Forster set foot in only one other club during his first journey (at Jodhpur), and that was as different from the Chandrapore Club as it could possibly be.

In 1912, the Residency Club at Indore was located in a low, red-brick bungalow with pillars around the front portico; a semi-circular driveway ran around the front of the building, while the back side contained a small garden which was bounded by a low wall to protect the flowers from the dust raised on the adjacent Bombay-Agra road.[58] This road was the dividing line between the Residency area and the "native quarter," and it is interesting to speculate whether the relative lack of privacy was one of the reasons for the abandonment of these quarters. In any case, during the First World War the Club moved to a larger building with more spacious grounds about a mile away, on the far side of the Residency compound; when Forster returned to Indore in 1921, it was to this second location that he came on the few occasions when he was invited down from Dewas.[59] The Residency Club at Indore differed from the one in Forster's novel in permitting carefully selected Indians inside the premises as guests, nearly all of them princes of neighboring native states. One of these was the Rajah of Dewas Senior, whom Forster first met at the club ("On the 23rd I was in the club at Indore with Major Luard who mentioned my name aloud, when up sprung a bright and tiny young Indian, and wrung me by both hands. This was the Rajah of Dewas").[60] But these meager concessions to local royalty were hardly indications of an enlightened attitude toward Indians: not until 1945 were Indians admitted as members—and then only by default.[61] The prevailing club attitude was one of racial exclusivity based on willful ignorance of Indian social customs. Here is Forster's characterization of this narrow thinking in his fictional club:

> But then the club moved slowly; it still declared that few Moham-
> medans and no Hindus would eat at an Englishman's table, and
> that all Indian ladies were in impenetrable purdah. Individually it
> knew better; as a club it declined to change.[62]

To its members the Anglo-Indian club was a refuge from the implacably threatening world around it; the club walls sheltered them from people and places they did not understand, and this isolation intensified the already strong sense of being in exile in a foreign land. Inside the club, a great effort was made to re-create as closely as possible the atmosphere of England: one of the most effective ways to do this was to deny India's existence by forbidding entrance to Indians. In times of political unrest, the club was a fortress against "the natives" and represented the one firm principle of order in a chaotic environment. Forster's account of the Chandrapore Club just before Aziz's trial gives a perceptive picture of this frame of mind:

> People drove into the club with studious calm—the jog-trot of
> country gentlefolk between green hedgerows, for the natives must
> not suspect that they were agitated. They exchanged the usual
> drinks, but everything tasted different and then they looked out at
> the palisade of cactuses stabbing the purple throat of the sky; they
> realised that they were thousands of miles from any scenery they
> understood. The club was fuller than usual, and several parents
> had brought their children into the rooms reserved for adults,
> which gave the air of the Residency at Lucknow.[63]

With its neat garden and comforting atmosphere, the club represents all that is secure and meaningful. It is fitting that when Fielding violates the solidarity of "the herd," his punishment is exclusion from the club. Forster particularly disliked this side of Anglo-Indian life, and his memory of the Residency Club at Indore inspired the caustic version of club life in *A Passage to India*.

Englishmen in Exile: Patiala and Jodhpur

Forster was troubled by what he saw of Anglo-Indians in his travels around India. He found their manners frequently offensive and was unable to relax among people who were so stubbornly insular and incurious about an environment he himself found enchanting. Yet he recognized that many of their unpleasant qualities expressed the profound discontent of a people in exile. The tangible sense of melancholy that pervaded many Anglo-Indian households did not escape Forster's notice; in the novel he describes·the club members after the singing of "God Save the King" as "strengthened to resist another day."[64] Other outside observers of Anglo-India also discerned a joylessness in the people—one Indian literary critic offers this perception:

> The sense of their being "exiles" in a foreign land seldom deserts the English in India. Separation from their friends and families and the varied, intellectual, and civilized life of the West; the constant journeyings; the oppressiveness of the Indian climate in summer; the monotony of official life and the feeling that doing one's duty in India is a thankless job—all these impart to the most frivolous novel a note of sadness.[65]

Forster glimpsed this sadness on a very brief visit to Patiala, a small but wealthy native state in the Punjab where his host was Edmund Candler, a well-known journalist and author of several popular novels on India. Candler was a teacher at the Government College at Patiala; this post did allow him a little time for his writing but was nonetheless essentially a stultifying and isolated experience for a well-educated Englishman with diverse interests. Forster found him rather depressed and self-pitying, and sensed that here was a good mind going to seed in one of North India's most stagnant native states:

> C.'s [Candler's] mind is serviceable and appreciative, but lacks fineness: Daily Mail correspondent in Tibet where he lost an arm, and writes for Blackwood. Would chuck Patiala for literature but for his wife; returning we found her back from the Skating Rink.

Talk of Court intrigues and the brave and worthless Maharajah:
fourth wife lately.[66]

Forster was struck by how little intellectual stimulation there
was for Candler in Patiala when he was taken around several
rooms of the Maharajah's palace and shown a bizarre hodge-
podge of tasteless European knickknacks and gaudy silver acces-
sories:

> Drove with C. to his work—the vast red pillared college is a bastard
> but imposing. Viewed rooms, kitchens and lavatories with his clerk
> who took me on to Fort where I saw silver howdahs and carriages
> and a silver room which went to the Durbar, and liked some chairs
> whose arms were horseheads of silver or gilt silver. Maharaja has
> bought many little statues in Paris—Dante, *très mignon,* delicate
> vases, eggs which open and have naked ladies inside. These are
> covered with dusters and placed in dark corners. And the usual ar-
> mour. In the inner Fort sit many Ranis, intriguing to the sound of
> a gramophone which penetrated the windowless walls.[67]

More pleasant was an excursion on horseback with Candler into
the countryside:

> Rode through city and to Bir—a level preserve half under water:
> cantered and galloped and have left a part of me doing it: onward
> winding between scrub and never jerking or stopping with black
> buck running before me and peacocks and wild boar flying: once a
> Nilghai. Rain. C. said I rode hopefully.[68]

Like Forster, Candler appreciated the physical beauty of the Indian countryside, but this was not sufficient solace for the loneliness and alienation of his life at Patiala. Candler's novels on
India, spanning the years 1900 to 1922, became increasingly
pessimistic about the chances for understanding between English and Indians: his last novels are pervaded by gloom and the
poignant malaise of a man who has spent too much of his life in
exile. Benita Parry summarizes Candler's fiction in these terms:

> Perhaps Candler's major attainment is his account of how un-
> comfortable an environment India was to the white man. His con-
> sciousness of the British as displaced persons in Asia was inten-
> sified with the development of political unrest when a people
> whom they had seen as docile, supine and incompetent were

challenging their mission to India. . . . . Candler's adventure with India led him to despair of intimacy on the human plane and drove him back to the lines of his own people.[69]

In sharp contrast to Patiala was Jodhpur, a dramatic sandstone city in the heart of the Rajputana desert which Forster came to only five days after leaving Patiala. In Jodhpur, Forster found an Anglo-Indian community living in harmony and mutual respect with Indians: all the unpleasant characteristics he had come to expect in small English enclaves in India were absent, making his stay in Jodhpur exceptionally enjoyable. Writing of Jodhpur's Anglo-Indian residents after his return to England in 1914, Forster elaborated on the human qualities he had found so attractive there:

> They had none of the indifference to their surroundings that is considered good form elsewhere. They loved the city and the people living in it, and an outsider's enthusiasm, instead of boring them, appeared to give pleasure. Men and women, they shared the same club as the Indians, and under its gracious roof the "racial question" had been solved—not by reformers, who only accent the evils they define, but by the genius of the city, which gave everyone something to work for and think about. I had heard of this loyalty at the other end of the peninsula—it was avowedly rare. But no one had described the majesty that inspired it—the air blowing in from the desert, the sand and the purple stones, the hills with quarries and tanks beneath, and the palace-fortress on the highest hill, an amazement forever, a dragon's crown.[70]

In Forster's mind, the correlation between the human atmosphere of a place and its physical setting was always close: to him Jodhpur's beauty seemed intimately linked to the harmonious state of human relations there. This desert city, dominated by an enormous fort built in the fifteenth century, is comprised of winding streets with houses featuring delicately carved balconies and intricate ornamental grillwork. An unusually large number of older houses has been preserved into the present century, and one noted scholar of Indian architecture has described the old city as "a fascinating dream of beauty."[71] This dreamlike quality entranced many English travelers. One was

Yvonne Fitzroy, who visited Jodhpur in 1923 as the private secretary to Lady Reading, the wife of the Viceroy. Her impressions echo Forster's sheer delight at this improbable fortress:

> All our forts have hitherto been dead forts—or rather deserted—and the peculiar charm of Jodhpur lay in the fact that it was very much alive, but with a life that was centuries old . . . the ascent is very steep, and gorgeous richly embroidered dhoolies (a long carrying-chair slung on a pole) waited to carry us up the narrow stone-paved causeway, between a high wall on one hand and the eight stories of the palace rising sheer from the rock on the other. From the tremendous masonry beside us to the lovely carved balconies and windows hanging far above against the narrow ribbon of blue sky, it was perfect.[72]

In Jodhpur Forster's hosts were all employees of the Jodhpur-Bikaner Railway, which ran between the two desert cities. He was taken along a new line of rails by the resident engineer, M. Spartali, and given a look at the striking desert scenery along the way:

> S. took me up his new line on a trolley. Four men, each two ran 50 steps and then rested: lifting it from the line when the train came. We passed Mandor and came to a wall running towards a promontory: through there the desert, untouched and untouchable, amethystine. Hot sun, cool wind through the cactuses and having crossed the purple rocks came sand and the line grew unsteady and stopped: there are no more rails.[73]

This railway which trails off into nothingness in the desert is an emblem of the English in India and recalls Forster's characterization in the novel of England's presence in India:

> The triumphant machine of civilization may suddenly hitch and be immobilized into a car of stone, and at such moments the destiny of the English seems to resemble their predecessors', who also entered the country with intent to refashion it, but were in the end worked into its pattern and covered with its dust.[74]

Time and again in *A Passage to India* the orderly workings of English civilization are thwarted by the implacable Indian terrain. The symmetry so dear to rational men is lost in the formlessness of the Indian earth, just as the neat pattern of railway ties in Jodhpur ends in an amorphous expanse of sand.

Forster's six-day visit to Jodhpur is notable because it suggested to him a new standard for human relations in the colonial context, a standard that had formerly been only a vague notion in his mind. He wrote that it was "as if each race had made concessions"[75] to the other's peculiarities, thereby creating a new basis for friendship and understanding. This sense of harmony was epitomized for Forster by an Englishman in Jodhpur whom he knew only slightly, George Goyder, the chief finance officer of the Jodhpur-Bikaner Railway.[76] Goyder, who was leaving Jodhpur the next day for another post, took Forster with him on his final ride around the city, and the novelist was moved by the affection and respect shown to Goyder by the Indians who came out to say goodbye. Forster's diary records his own emotions at this poignant scene:

> G. took me the drive, promised so long, in the evening, too sad to speak, and taking farewell of the city he has helped and loved. More charming than any, and prosperous. White raised loggias with coloured turbans in them, new market place, revealing Fort, tank edged by temple wall, two deep fissures under the Fort full of water and that of fish that Brahmins fed, obscene figures ready for Holi—he showed me all, and when we stood on a gateway, where the Fort lashes into the houses with a rocky tail, and saw the city tossing purple and golden with the desert beyond, I felt also to be losing something, for if I ever see Jodhpur again it will never be thus. Here at last is the perfect Anglo-Indian, seeing the faults of the Indians but not brooding over them till he stifles enthusiasm and love: no wonder people crowded round the car to say how fond they were of him.[77]

In this new acquaintance Forster found an honest and straightforward Englishman whose attempt to meet Indians on an equal basis had been rewarded with love and respect. Just as the Indian earth in his novel so often mirrors human affairs both bad and good, so in Jodhpur Forster found the positive state of personal relations reflected in the beauty of the surroundings.

Journey's End: Hyderabad and Aurangabad

The cities of Hyderabad and Aurangabad were the last
places that Forster saw before returning to Bombay for his ship
to England. The first was the capital city of the richest and largest native state, ruled over by a hereditary Muslim dynasty that
had made the name of Hyderabad synonymous with luxury and
splendor: the ruler in Forster's time, Sir Osman Ali, Nizam of
Hyderabad, was often called "the richest man in the world." [78]
Forster found Hyderabad a refreshing change from the chaos of
North India, and his kaleidoscopic account of a day of sightseeing with English friends is suffused with quiet pleasure:

> City, though neither well built nor picturesque, has an air. Over a
> river and through a bad modern gate one drives straight to Char
> Minar whence four roads. Splashes of scarlet—fez, coats bespat-
> tered for Holi. Soldiers, elephants, holy men in balconies. May en-
> tered shops and squatted to bargain. Very nice with people. To
> mosque after sunset—a cathedral with side out. Through a gate
> among houses. Delicacy and mystery—unlike North India. Un-
> pleasant men stopped me entering though my shoes were off.
> Nizam's tomb in forecourt—sensibly meagre.—Moonlit dinner on
> a cluster of rocks in the tank: Miss Carter came, a fat nice girl, and
> we were very merry. It was difficult to land and to fix the boat—
> very easily would it slip into deep water—and the rocks were slip-
> pery yet rough. Lovely it was to eat in the cool with the tropical
> shore edging the water dimly. [79]

There are obvious antecedents here of scenes in *A Passage to
India*—a misunderstanding over shoes at a mosque (Aziz and
Mrs. Moore) and an excursion by boat that proves perilous,
recalling the capsizing of the Fieldings' boat at Mau.

Even in Hyderabad, Forster became entangled in the mesh
of Anglo-India. His diary records a conversation presaging the
comments in Simla and Delhi when the novel appeared in 1924
and also exemplifying the Anglo-Indian passion for labeling
things in order to render them comprehensible:

> Mrs. G. —"What sort of novels do you write? Are they nice?" —"I
> can answer that—no." —"Oh I see they are modern." —"Yes, that

is the alternative." —"Problem novels, I suppose. Well, for my own part I think there are no problems left—all have been written about." —"Yes, they are old, but the writer's young." —"Well, I don't like problems."[80]

This same woman also spoke unkindly of an Indian family that Forster later became quite intimate with, the Hydaris, who had served in the Nizam's government for generations. Sir Muhammad Akbar Hydari was high up in the Hyderabad civil service and did a great deal to modernize the state's finances. This friendship lasted many years: when Forster returned to Hyderabad in 1945, he stayed with Sir Akbar Hydari, the son of the man he had met in 1913. One of the most memorable things about the Hydaris was that Forster was permitted to meet and speak with Hydari's wife, who no longer observed the seclusion of the purdah. He remarks in this diary that Mrs. Hydari is "the first Mahommedan lady I've seen."[81] His novel is pervaded by an awareness of the changing status of India's Muslim women—Aziz inveighs against purdah; some of Chandrapore's purdah women undergo a fast in support of Aziz during his trial; and Hamidullah, who has imbibed the liberal notions of the West during his undergraduate days at Cambridge, laments to Aziz his own wife's slowness in shedding her traditional isolation:

"... far too much nonsense still goes on among our ladies. They pretended at the time of your trial they would give up purdah; indeed, those of them who can write composed a document to that effect, and now it ends in humbug. You know how deeply they all respect Fielding, but not one of them has seen him. My wife says she will, but always when he calls there is some excuse—she is not feeling well, she is ashamed of the room, she has no nice sweets to offer him, only Elephant's Ears, and if I say Elephant's Ears are Mr. Fielding's favourite sweet, she replies that he will know how badly hers are made, so she cannot see him on their account."[82]

One must conclude that Forster's sensitivity to this issue came almost exclusively from his second journey, when the removal of purdah had gone much further than in 1913. Forster did return to Hyderabad several times in 1921 and found the Muslim community there much altered, both internally and also as a response to the rapid changes in post–World War I social values.

Some 250 miles north of Hyderabad is the smaller city of Aurangabad, which had briefly been the capital of the Mughal Empire under Aurangzeb in the seventeenth century. In 1913, Aurangabad was a center of Maratha culture and served as the administrative headquarters for the northernmost portion of Hyderabad State, whose inhabitants spoke Marathi rather than the Urdu and Telegu of the more populous central region. Here Forster had come to visit with an Indian friend from Cambridge, Abu Saeed Mirza,[83] now a magistrate of the Hyderabad government. Forster recorded in his diary several experiences from Aurangabad which reappear, some of them barely altered, in *A Passage to India*.

The most striking of these involves a horseback ride into the countryside with Abu Saeed Mirza: it is clearly the inspiration for the crucial scene at the end of Forster's novel in which Aziz and Fielding go riding and discuss India's future:

> Kept quietish all day, but rode in evening, and most successfully. Horse played no tricks and we trotted and cantered over open country to Mahratta village. Saeed burst out against the English. "It may be 50 or 500 years but we shall turn you out." He hates us far more than his brother does. Horse curvetting all the time in the sunset. Very jolly. Patches of green among the barren—we rode from one to another to admire. Horse played no tricks: S. made his play—an amiable show-off. Energy and sense at the bottom.[84]

The casual tone here belies the considerable impression this made on Forster: he is clearly in sympathy with his friend's sentiments, seeing "energy and sense" at the core of this attitude toward the English. Forster takes Saeed's little speech and expands it in the novel into Aziz's outburst on British rule; the spirit and vitality of this young Muslim who no longer wants or needs the approval of foreigners is probably taken directly from Abu Saeed Mirza. Like Aziz, Saeed feels affection for his English friend, but is no longer willing to know him on unequal terms. Forster sees Saeed as a direct descendant of the Mughals and their penchant for grandiose gestures, and he presents Aziz in the same light. Another riding excursion mentioned in the diary evokes a tangle of related associations between the romantic glories of the past and the realities of the present:

> After ten we rode, the horse became an odd shape and I fell off on my right-hand bottom. "I am thankful to God it was no more," said S., but is callous and sensible about illness. We went to a lovely Mohammedan shrine, but I was too shaken to appreciate it and my drawers were coming down. I remember small buildings divided by pavements and flowers with a trough of a tank beneath them. —On to the Golden Palace, a ruin under the hills, but it was locked and twilight; rode slowly to the "Taj": saw a light in a mosque and found none on arrival: were tangled in steep ground. Romantic— the ruins are endless, far flung among the lovely undulations, and the dried-up fountains touch imagination. Not even at Fatehpur did I feel the vanished Moghul Empire thus. S. is a remnant of that empire: many a young blood must have jogged through the evening before him.[85]

Another detail from Aurangabad appearing in the novel is Saeed's house just outside the city, where Forster was taken to stay by his friend:

> Saeed drove up as I was having a bath and took me to stop with him in a lovely wooden hall: two rows of triple arches, which, like the internal pavilions, were painted blue; my bedroom—half the height—was to right, servants to left. Square tank of green water.[86]

Fielding's house in the book is described as having "a very beautiful room, opening into the garden through three high arches of wood,"[87] and Aziz calls the attention of Mrs. Moore and Adela Quested to the carvings and the blue-painted pillars in the interior.[88] In Aurangabad Forster also noticed a young man working the *punkah* (fan) in Saeed's courtroom ("Punkah boy, seated at end of table, had the impassivity of Atropos").[89] This figure is recreated in the same image in the novel's courtroom scene: "he seemed apart from human destinies, a male fate, a winnower of souls."[90]

The principal sightseeing Forster undertook was to the famous caves at Ellora, yet his diary indicates remarkably little reaction to these great masterpieces of early Indian art. He wrote about Ellora and the nearby Ajanta caves in later years when he reviewed several books on Indian art for English journals, but the comments in his diary on Ellora, though full of wonderment and praise, are terse:

> Ellora. Kailas at sunset. More amazing than anything in a land where much amazes. Supporting cornice of blackened monsters—elephants, griffons and tigers who rend. The great mild face of a goddess, doing cruelty, fades into the pit-wall.[91]

Forster's relative lack of enthusiasm for the most renowned sights in India—the Taj Mahal in Agra, the Khajuraho temples, the Ajanta and Ellora caves—is curious, and ought to be considered in relation to those sights which did inspire and excite him—Jodhpur Fort, the deserted city of Mandu in central India, and the little-known countryside around Chhatarpur and Dewas. Perhaps his lack of response to the most famous monuments relates to the consistency with which expectations are thwarted in India: this is a prominent theme in the novel (one instance is Adela's enthusiastic preface to the sunrise that doesn't come) and it may well be that Forster was most receptive to India in moments when he held no preconceptions to mar his enjoyment. In any case, Aurangabad marked the last stop before Bombay in Forster's first Indian journey, and he departed amid garlands and "unforgettable kindness."[92] Even a modest final expectation—the purchase of a gift for his friend Saeed—was frustrated, ending his first passage to India with the appropriate muddle and memories of loving hospitality:

> *April 2.* Travelled Intermediate Manmad-Bombay. Boat twelve hours early. Fearful scuffle to get off—couldn't get Saeed cakes at Mongini's. It's as if I am to do nothing for him, however slight. "The accounts of friends are written in the heart" is his explanation.[93]

chapter 4

Timeless India:
The Barabar Caves

The physical center of Forster's novel is located in the Marabar Hills and the caves they contain: the crucial action in the plot takes place there, and the presence of the Marabar echoes again and again throughout the book. For Forster, the caves represent an India entirely separate from that of the British or the Indians—they symbolize the timelessness of the Indian earth and its enduring qualities, for the Marabar Hills are pointedly described as "immemorial"[1] and "older than anything in the world."[2] The Marabar is the ultimate embodiment of the insignificance of human beings in an ominous landscape that mocks their notions of self-importance. So removed are these hills from the scope of human endeavor that they stand alone and untouched, too forbidding for even the various ascetics who have encountered them:

> There is something unspeakable in these outposts. They are like nothing else in the world, and a glimpse of them makes the breath catch. They rise abruptly, insanely, without the proportion that is kept by the wildest hills elsewhere, they bear no relation to anything dreamt or seen. To call them "uncanny" suggests ghosts, and they are older than all spirit. Hinduism has scratched and plastered a few rocks, but the shrines are unfrequented, as if pilgrims, who generally seek the extraordinary, had here found too much of it. Some saddhus did once settle in a cave, but they were smoked out, and even Buddha, who must have passed this way down to the Bo Tree of Gya, shunned a renunciation more complete than his own, and has left no legend of struggle or victory in the Marabar.[3]

The sheer isolation of the caves from the other Indias of Forster's novel is emphasized by the failure of the various characters to comprehend or describe them in any way. Aziz, a Muslim, is bewildered and out of place at the Marabar: "His ignorance became evident, and was really rather a drawback. In spite of his gay, confident talk, he had no notion how to treat this particular aspect of India; he was lost in it, without Professor Godbole, like themselves."[4] But the Brahman can do no better when he is asked at Fielding's garden party to describe the caves: he can only say that they are not like the caves at Elephanta, not "immensely holy"[5] (as Aziz suggests to him), not ornamented in any way. In the end the assembled company is left "further than ever from discovering what, if anything, was extraordinary about the Marabar Caves."[6] When Ronny, the last word in British efficiency and omniscience, is asked if he has been to the caves, he blusters unconvincingly, "No, but I know all about them, naturally."[7] The caves are simply beyond the powers of human understanding, and they cause Mrs. Moore to have her negative vision of human relations which is so central to the novel's meaning.

Forster has stated explicitly in the Everyman edition of *A Passage to India* that the Marabar Caves are based on the Barabar Caves in Bihar, about sixteen miles north of Gaya. The author visited these caves in late January of 1913, and his diary suggests that the journey to the caves in the novel comes directly from his own experience. Forster's account of the barren and impoverished Bihar countryside emphasizes the starkness of the terrain and the sinister quality of the approach to the Barabar Hills:

> Left at 6.30.   After one glimpse the raw greyness. Agrawala, Mahmoud, and brother saw me off at Bela. Nawab Imdad Imam and nephews and elephants met me. . . . Six-spot beetle killed near our tent—more deadly than a snake. Country untilled—population wretched, graves dug open by animals. A whitewashed ⋀⋀ was not a grave but the breasts of Parvati, and the toddy palms, cut again and again, were to me those breasts run dry. Where there were fields they were thus irrigated. Forked branch, pole, or mud tower, over which another pole was laid. At one end of pole string and bucket descending into well. At other end counterpoise of mud. Men pull up the counterpoise, release it and tip raised bucket into a runnel. These antennae wave among the fields, the men often invisible.[8]

The abrupt quality of the writing here is uncharacteristic of Forster's diary entries: when he recreates this scene in the novel, the writing is naturally more polished, but the harshness of the setting has been preserved and the atmosphere is much the same:

> The train . . . wobbled away through the fields, turning its head this way and that like a centipede. And the only other movement to be seen was a movement as of antennae, really the counterpoises of the wells which rose and fell on their pivots of mud over the plain and dispersed a feeble flow of water. . . . As the elephant moved towards the hills (the pale sun had by this time saluted them to the base, and pencilled shadows down their creases) a new quality occurred, a spiritual silence which invaded more senses than the ear. Life went on as usual, but had no consequences, that is to say, sounds did not echo or thoughts develop. Everything seemed cut off at its root, and therefore infected with illusion. For instance, there were some mounds by the edge of the track, low, serrated, and touched with whitewash. What were these mounds—graves, breasts of the goddess Parvati? . . . Nothing was explained, and yet there was no romance.[9]

Forster's diary does not actually describe the caves, but it is clear that they remained etched in his mind, for the caves in the novel, although different in some details, are in essence the Barabar Caves:

> The caves are readily described. A tunnel eight feet long, five feet high, three feet wide, leads to a circular chamber about twenty feet in diameter. This arrangement occurs again and again throughout the group of hills, and this is all, this is a Marabar Cave. Having seen one such cave, having seen two, having seen three, four, fourteen, twenty-four, the visitor returns to Chandrapore uncertain whether he has had an interesting experience or a dull one or any experience at all. He finds it difficult to discuss the caves, or to keep them apart in his mind, for the pattern never varies, and no carving, not even a bees'-nest or a bat, distinguishes one from another. . . . They are dark caves. Even when they open towards the sun, very little light penetrates down the entrance tunnel into the circular chamber. There is little to see, and no eye to see it, until the visitor arrives for his five minutes, and strikes a match. Immediately another flame rises in the depths of the rock and moves towards the surface like an imprisoned spirit; the walls of the circular chamber have been most marvellously polished.

. . . Only the wall of the circular chamber has been polished thus.
The sides of the tunnel are left rough, they impinge as an after-
thought upon the internal perfection. An entrance was necessary,
so mankind made one.[10]

Descriptions of the Barabar Caves by travelers and
archaeologists reveal several important differences between
these and the caves in Forster's novel: there are only seven
caves in the Barabar (not the twenty-four or more that Forster
mentions), and the entrances to some have fragments of or-
namentation. Furthermore, the Barabar Caves are not all iden-
tical, but have internal differences—some contain stone plat-
forms that once supported images of deities, and the
arrangement of the chambers (some circular, some oval) and
tunnels varies slightly from cave to cave. The first account of
the Barabar Caves and surrounding hills is probably that of
Francis Buchanan-Hamilton, who made a survey of the region
for the British in 1811, just over a century before Forster's
visit.[11] Buchanan-Hamilton tells in his journal of the initial
foray into the hills:

I went about ten miles, but by a very circuitous route, to Keyoa Dol
(Kawa Dol). I proceeded first south-east about three miles until I
left to my right a village and old mud fort named Duraut
(Dharaut). I then inclined more to the south about 2 miles, until I
came to the east end of Beyok (Bhekh), a detached part of an exceedingly rugged ridge of granite among which are only some
stunted bushes and climbers. . . . It does not consist of great
rocks but of immense irregular blocks. . . . I came to the west
corner of a low ridge adjoining to the west end of the Burabur
pahar (Barabar Hills) the highest and largest of this cluster, and I
passed between this low ridge and another detached hill farther
west. The north face of Burabur is not nearly so rugged as the
northern ridge, but is only covered by stunted bushes, but on the
south it is exceedingly rough and contains some immense precipi-
tous rocks.[12]

This recalls the atmosphere of the Marabar, particularly the
rocky terrain studded with thorn bushes that nearly kills Adela
Quested after her panic in the cave. Buchanan-Hamilton goes
on to describe the approach to the caves and the caves themselves in meticulous detail:

After breakfast I went to visit what is called the Satgar, or
seven houses, situated towards the east end of Burabur hill. . . .
Advancing west a little way, with an old tank and a small level on
my right and a ridge of solid granite on my left, I soon came to a
door in the latter facing the north, where a high peak crowned by a
temple of Mahadeva bounds the plain in that direction. The rock at
this door has been cut perpendicular, leaving a small projection at
each side some way from the door. Before this door have been
some small buildings of brick. The door leads into a chamber, polished like that of Nagarjuni and equally devoid of ornament. It is
about 16 feet from east to west and 40 from north to south, and
about seven high to the spring of the arch. At its west end is a platform about a foot high and three feet broad. . . . This cave is
called *Karn Chaupar* or the house of Karna. This Karna is supposed to be the brother of Yudishtir, who passed some time here as
a hermit.

Passing round the west end of this ridge to its south side, you
come to two doors. The first or most western is plain, and has on
each side a few words engraved. It leads into a chamber of about
the size with that called *Karna Chaupar*. At its east side is a small
niche. At its west end is a door in the wall, which is convex, and
over the door is a kind of cornice. The door leads into a circular
chamber, arched above like the others, and polished in the same
manner. The floor of these chambers contained about a foot of
dirty water and mud. This cave is properly called Satgar and is
supposed to have been built by Sudama, brother of Krishna. The
other door east from the above has been somewhat but very rudely
ornamented, as will appear from the drawing. Under the arch
above the door is an inscription of considerable length. It seems to
have been intended to have formed two chambers similar to those
of Satgar, but although both have been excavated, neither has
been completed nor polished except in a few parts. This is supposed to have been the abode of *Lomus Rishi*, . . . a hairy saint of
these remote times.[13]

This early account of the Barabar Caves is closely paralleled by
modern ones, which all stress the rugged setting and the extraordinary workmanship of the polished inner chambers.[14]

Forster also visited three other sets of caves in India well
known for their paintings and carvings, but none made the lasting impression upon him that the Barabar Caves did. His trips
to the caves at Ellora, Elephanta, and Aurangabad are mentioned in the diary only in passing and nothing is said of any

echo like the one he encountered in the Barabar Caves. A recent visit (1976) to these caves revealed that they do indeed contain a remarkably powerful echo exactly like the one in Forster's novel. Visits to the Ajanta, Ellora, Elephanta, and Aurangabad caves turned up nothing more than faint resonances in the inner chambers of certain caves, but experiments inside the Karna Chaupar and Lomas Rishi caves at Barabar produced long echoes which Forster has described with uncanny accuracy. Every footstep resounds for at least several seconds, and vocalized sounds, whether low-pitched or high-pitched, produce a deep, rumbling echo which sometimes lasts up to half a minute. The echo in the novel is presented in precise terms that leave no doubt as to the model for it: "Whatever is said, the same monotonous noise replies, and quivers up and down the walls until it is absorbed into the roof. 'Boum' is the sound as far as the human alphabet can express it, or 'bou-oum,' or 'ou-boum,'—utterly dull. Hope, politeness, the blowing of a nose, the squeak of a boot, all produce 'boum.' "[15]

The most vivid description of Forster's journey to the Barabar is contained in a letter written to his mother and aunt:

> On one side the rock comes down smooth and rounded like an inverted saucer and plunges into the earth of the plain. Beyond this—alas some way—were the other hills—and at their feet in a grove of palms, the tents were pitched. But breakfast—mockery of a name!—was not ready, and it was suggested we should visit the Buddhist caves while it was cooking. Here again were rocks, steps had been cut up them and in much heat and intense emptiness I climbed. The caves are cut out of solid granite: a small square door way and an oval hall inside. . . . One of them has a frieze of elephants over the door, but in the rest the only decoration is the fine Pali inscriptions on the sides of the entrance tunnel. Standing inside one sees them in the strong sunlight, and beyond the view. We lit candles which showed the grain of the granite and its reds and greys. The nephews [of Forster's host] also tried to wake the echoes, but whatever was said and in whatever voice the cave only returned a dignified roar. . . .[16]

Forster's strange and vaguely unsettling experience here is most likely the inspiration for Mrs. Moore's awful moment of terror and negation, a moment which echoes throughout the grim business of Aziz's supposed crime and the trial which follows. Only when Mrs. Moore is leaving India and the palm trees in Bombay harbor tell her, "So you thought an echo was India; you took the Marabar Caves as final?" [17] does the evil of that moment begin to dissipate, and only in the life-affirming chaos of the final section of the book is the message of the Marabar put into perspective. For Forster, the caves and their echo symbolize all that is evil in the universe; for him, this evil is most dangerous in the realm of human relationships. Hence Mrs. Moore's transformation from an outgoing woman seeking fruitful personal contacts to a "withered priestess" [18] uttering baleful and mysterious prophecies. But Forster has referred elsewhere to Mrs. Moore's oracular pronouncements as the overreaction of a "tiresome old woman." [19] Her glimpse into the abyss is similar to that of Kurtz in Conrad's "Heart of Darkness," but it is far too prosaic ("no one could romanticize the Marabar because it robbed infinity and eternity of their vastness") [20] to call for "The horror! The horror!" Forster deliberately undercuts the message of the caves by admonishing his reading audience, "Visions are supposed to entail profundity, but—Wait till you get one, dear reader! The abyss also may be petty, the serpent of eternity made of maggots. . . ." [21] This illustrates Forster's ultimate faith in the power of human relations to overcome the darker forces of the universe: the final section of the novel, which describes the birth festival of the god Krishna, reasserts the primacy of "Love, the Beloved Republic." [22] This attitude can be seen in Forster's summary comments on the Ellora Caves: "Morning, I revisited Caves alone . . . their impression is already fading, I think because there is no beauty and I do not believe in the devil, whose palace they are. They are Satan's masterpieces to terrify others: the moustached Buddhas are not glaring at me." [23] Thus, critics who have presented the Marabar Caves as Forster's final grim summation of the state of human relations have neglected an important aspect of the novel—and they have ignored the powerful significance of the book's final section. [24]

chapter 5

Second Passage: Dewas, 1921

Between Visits: The Years 1913–21

A Passage to India was begun in the enthusiastic aftermath of Forster's 1912–13 journey to India. By his own account, chapters I through IV of the novel (ending with Godbole's song at Fielding's garden party) were written between his return home in April 1913 and the end of that year; small fragments of chapters VII, XII, and XIV were also written in this period.[1] But this was as far as Forster could go: January of 1914 found him "stuck"[2] on his Indian novel, and he put it aside. Speaking to an Italian audience in 1959, Forster described the nature of the "writer's block" which had suddenly interrupted his progress in 1913:

> The genesis of the book is worth mentioning. I began the book after my 1912 visit, wrote half a dozen chapters of it and stuck. I was clear about the chief characters and the racial tension, had visualized the scenes, and had foreseen that something crucial would happen in the Marabar Caves. But I hadn't seen far enough.[3]

The novel lay untouched for nearly ten years: Forster resumed writing it only after his second voyage to India in 1921. Despite this particular impasse, his sense of personal involvement with India remained intact: indeed, ten of his twelve published pieces from 1914 deal directly with India or things Indian.[4] Several of these are more elaborately detailed versions of incidents already described in his diary;[5] the majority are reviews of books on varied Indian topics. Three more book reviews by Forster on India appeared in the next year, but all this literary activity came to a halt in the autumn of 1915 when he was sent to Egypt to serve with the Red Cross.

During Forster's almost four years in Alexandria, that supremely cosmopolitan city on the Mediterranean, his published writing was limited to a series of light and somewhat trivial pieces entitled "Alexandrian Vignettes." These appeared from time to time under the pseudonym "Pharos" in the *Egyptian Mail*, a newspaper for the city's English-speaking population.[6] But throughout this period he was also collecting the material on the history and cultures of Alexandria which eventually led to *Alexandria, A History and a Guide* (1922) and *Pharos and Pharillon* (1923). Forster kept in close touch with India during this time: he and Malcolm Darling exchanged frequent letters, and his correspondence with Syed Ross Masood continued unabated, as it did right up to the latter's death in 1937.[7] But India remained a distant idea until 1921, when Forster was suddenly thrust back into Indian life by an invitation from his friend, the Rajah (now Maharajah) of Dewas Senior.

India Again: Dewas, 1921

By 1921, life in Dewas was much changed: the seemingly cheerful and secure facade of the prince's domestic life had cracked irreparably in 1914, when his young wife sent word from her father's place in Kolhapur that she would never return to Dewas. Forster makes vague mention in *The Hill of Devi* of a purported scandal concerning the Rajah and one of his wife's handmaidens, but the reason for the rupture remains uncertain.[8] Whatever the cause, this marital struggle was the first of an extended series of misfortunes that plagued the young ruler and led to his downfall in the 1930s.

During the First World War, Dewas loyally supported the British war effort: afterwards the Rajah was upgraded to a Ma-

harajah in recognition of his services to England in that time of
crisis.[9] The advent of a new world order in Europe had little effect, however, on the internal operations of the state, and Dewas
remained under the control of a benevolent but incompetent au-
tocrat. One reform he instituted during the war in the spiritual
and social realm deserves mention: he opened the temples in
his state to all Hindus regardless of caste, and in this he was
well ahead of most of his fellow princes.

The failure of his marriage left the Maharajah insecure and
lonely: he had alienated the leading Maratha prince (Kolhapur),
and the Dewas court was known to be full of spies sent by his
angry father-in-law. He longed for someone to trust, someone
who, in Forster's words, "stood outside the court and its intrigues."[10] Turning instinctively to the one man whose affection
was unfailing, the prince wrote in 1920 to his old friend and
former tutor Malcolm Darling, then stationed in the Punjab,
and asked him to come to Dewas as his private secretary. Darling sent a long and understanding note declining the offer,
recommending instead Colonel William Leslie, an acquaintance
who had recently retired from a long career in Indian administration. The Maharajah followed this advice and invited the colonel, who arrived in the autumn of 1920; he proved a success,
but in February 1921 was forced to return to England on sick
leave. The Maharajah then wrote to his friend Morgan Forster,
asking him to come and take Leslie's place for several months
on a temporary basis. This invitation was gladly accepted, and
in *The Hill of Devi* Forster describes his reaction at the time:

> I was delighted. My fare both ways was to be paid. I was to get
> three hundred rupees per month. I was not clear what I was to do,
> nor when I came away was I clear what I had done. But off I went
> in the highest spirits, and on a P. & O. which was well up to
> sample: the voyage ended in "feverish gaiety, concerts, juggling
> with prizes, quarrels between elderly men over a game of deck
> quoits, special meeting of Sports Committee to adjudicate same"—
> in fact in all the things I was to escape. Dewas was not my only ob-
> jective. I wanted to see Masood, my Moslem friend, who was now
> Director of Education at Hyderabad.[11]

Forster's high hopes for this second journey to India were not disappointed, and in later years he described his Dewas experience as "the great opportunity of my life." [12]

In a letter to Masood telling of his new post, Forster is clearly excited at the prospect of seeing both India and his old friend again:

> Dearest SRM
>   I have the honour to inform you of a change of address. Kindly address your next letter not to Harnham Weybridge, but to Messrs. T. Cook, Bombay. I arrive there on the P. & O. Morea, due March 26th, then go to Messrs. Cook's office to see if there is a letter from you, and whether you have come to Bombay to meet me and taken us rooms at a Hotel. If you have not come (and it is unlikely, I know) I go on at once, or as soon as I can, to Dewas, where I am to stay in some capacity or other until August, and if when August comes I have not been murdered or fried, I shall come to stop with you, wherever you are. . . . So we shall meet this year dearest boy, and if I have luck in March. I have heaps that I long to hear. [13]

The vague notion that Forster had of his actual duties in Dewas was apparently shared by the Maharajah, who delegated to him a confusing array of responsibilities which bore no relation to his status as private secretary:

> The day after my arrival we had a bewildering interview and he assigned me my duties: gardens, tennis courts, motors, Guest House, Electric House. None of these had much to do with reading or writing, my supposed specialties. I had an office (hours 7–11 and 4–5). All the post was to pass through my hands. These were not the duties which I had expected or for which I was qualified, but this did not disturb us, and he spent most of the interview in writing me out lists of the dignitaries of state. [14]

Forster's quarters were located in the so-called "New Palace," an ugly, uncomfortable building which, though occupied, was still under construction. He notes with amusement the time-honored Indian inefficiency of this enterprise:

> We live amongst rubble and mortar, and excavations whence six men carry a basket of earth, no larger than a cat's, twenty yards once in five minutes. I have not yet discovered who loosens the earth, but am familiar with the boy who scrabbles it into the basket

with his fingers, the man who bears it on his head along the bottom of the chasm, the next man—very chatty and almost naked—who receives it from him and, merely turning round, places it on the head of No. 4. No. 4 begins the ascent, No. 5 continues it, and No. 6, who is immensely old, totters along the surface and drops the earth onto a heap which will have some day to be cleared away. And the basket has to be passed back. This is the scene under my window, but for acres around the soil is pitted with similar efforts, slabs of marble lie about, roads lead nowhere, costly fruit trees die for want of water, and I have discovered incidentally that £1,000 worth (figure accurate) of electric batteries lie in a room near at hand and will spoil unless fixed promptly.[15]

In the midst of all this chaos, Forster attempted to perform his strange collection of duties; given the obstacles, it is not surprising to find him writing an exasperated letter to Malcolm Darling several weeks after arriving:

I have been here for a fortnight, happy and worried at once. You will understand either state and laugh at the worries. So long as I am out for enjoyment, all contribute to it, but as soon as I try to serve Bapu Sahib [the Maharajah] or to make others serve him, I grasp a cloud. I am glad the arrangement is temporary only: ignorant of the language and of administration generally, I could not stop on here permanently. It would not have been fair. To check the idleness, incompetence and extravagance is quite beyond me. . . . If Fate in the form of any political party should ask Dewas a question, what answer could Dewas give?[16]

This note of frustration is repeatedly sounded in Forster's accounts of Dewas: his efforts to order things always seemed like "grasping a cloud." Clearly, the elusive atmosphere of Mau in the novel is an expression of Forster's feelings about Dewas. The whimsical description of his vain attempt to irrigate a bed of dying flowers is a microcosm of his Dewas experience in that each logical action is thwarted by the inherent confusion of the place, and in the end things remain unchanged:

I could never describe the muddle in this place. It is wheel within wheel. Pipes have been laid (for example) all down the flower border, and connected with an empty water tank, which stands on four legs and takes its share in spoiling our surroundings. It is connected—in its turn—with an almost empty well, and if there was any water in the well it would be raised into the tank by an electric pump of insufficient power to raise the water. You are not at the end of the chain yet, for the electric pump is connected with the Electric House which is only on at night, when all its energies are required for the Palace lighting. So there we are, and there are the flowers dying. I tried to raise the water from the well by bullocks, but only one pair could be found, and one of them was so ill that I sent it to Indore to the Hospital for Indisposed Cows. [17]

This environment in which there is no logical progression of cause and effect is difficult for the Western mind to grasp. Forster, however, was delighted to find himself for the first time unable to resort to the familiar English concepts that define and identify what does and does not exist.

Forster's later letters contain a note of bemused resignation: as he understood Dewas better, Forster was able to accept the "muddle" and disorder of the place as an essential part of its identity. The inherent absurdity of the administrative apparatus ceased to be a source of irritation and instead led him to consider the possibility that efficiency and order were not indispensable conditions of human existence. Behind the ostensible disarray of life at Dewas lay a refreshing vitality of spirit and a harmony between the inhabitants and their environment which Forster found admirable:

> these people were civilised, they were in accord with their surroundings, they were not struggling to adjust themselves against time, like the doomed westerner. I give their untidiness a good mark too. For the last ten years have taught me that tidy streets, spotless railway stations and penalties for rubbish are often the outward signs of clean-ups and cruelty. [18]

Forster's essential fair-mindedness is evident in his comments on Dewas: he is able to appreciate the positive features of life there without ignoring the shortcomings of the people, and his amusement at certain aspects of Indian life is never condescending. Rather than raging against the inevitable, Forster accepts situations that are beyond his control or comprehension. A good example of this is his attitude towards the lack of hygiene at Dewas:

Exactly what part the lower animals play in my system I know not yet, but it gave me a shock to meet a tortoise in the Krishna water works. It sat on the central slab—Vishnu himself no doubt. Now I drink soda water. Of course the tortoises of Indore have sat in that, but I do not see them, any more than I see the cooking of our Indian khana. It doesn't do to think. To follow the promptings of the eye and the imagination is quite complicated enough.[19]

He is willing to take India "as it is," unlike the visiting Political Agent who insists that a cow be milked in his presence— "otherwise he will feel uneasy about his tea."[20] Forster sees this as indicative of Anglo-India's determination to exclude all that is unfamiliar—hence the walled club, the closed shutters during the English play, and the steadfast rejection of Indian social and culinary traditions. This is the opposite of the Hindu world view, which emphasizes the incorporation of all the diverse elements of the universe, both animate and inanimate, into a harmonious whole.

A simple but nonetheless central theme of *A Passage to India* is the need for kindness and affection in human relations, particularly in the colonial context. Forster expresses this through Aziz, whose words to Fielding represent the core of the author's beliefs:

> "Mr. Fielding, no one can ever realize how much kindness we Indians need, we do not even realize it ourselves. But we know when it has been given. We do not forget, though we may seem to. Kindness, more kindness, and even after that more kindness. I assure you it is the only hope."[21]

This vital theme is derived from Forster's friendship with the ruler of Dewas, whom he always referred to as "H. H." (His Highness) or "Bapu Sahib." Despite the atmosphere of palace intrigue and political infighting, the Maharajah was always responsive to those who showed him genuine kindness:

> Affection, all through his chequered life, was the only force to which Bapu Sahib responded. It did not always work, but without it nothing worked. Affection and its attendants of human warmth and instinctive courtesy—when they were present his heart awoke and dictated his actions.[22]

Unlike most of his race in India, Forster felt that affection was the essential ingredient in personal relations: the cruelty and coldness of the Anglo-Indians in his novel are deliberately juxtaposed with the easy familiarity between Aziz and Fielding. Mrs. Moore's encounter with Aziz in the mosque is another instance of natural sympathy between two disparate human beings. But Adela Quested's recantation, which after all saves Aziz, is rejected by the Indians because they can discern no love or warmth behind her action. Forster describes Hamidullah's incomprehension:

> while relieving the Oriental mind, she had chilled it, with the result that he could scarcely believe she was sincere, and indeed from his standpoint she was not. For her behavior rested on cold justice and honesty; she had felt, while she recanted, no passion of love for those whom she had wronged. Truth is not truth in that exacting land unless there go with it kindness and more kindness and kindness again, unless the word that was with God is also God. And the girl's sacrifice—so creditable according to Western notions—was rightly rejected, because, though it came from her heart, it did not include her heart.[23]

Both this and Forster's observations on the Maharajah's instinct for kindness illustrate his understanding of the subtleties of interracial relationships in the Raj. He saw that the long years of contact with the British had made Indians acutely sensitive to any insincerity or condescension in the way they were treated— hence Hamidullah's shrewd appraisal of Adela's sudden change of mind. Early in his acquaintance with India, Malcolm Darling had noticed the same thing:

> They [Indians] were quick too to detect any touch of hollowness in such sympathy as was offered them. For example, of one Lieutenant-Governor, it was said, in a typical mixture of English and Hindustani—'AFFABILITY BAHUT, MAGAR TRUE SYMPATHY KUCHH NAHIN'—great affability, but of true sympathy not a jot.[24]

Forster's stay in Dewas was the most emotionally satisfying time he spent in India: he was instantly loved and treated warmly, though a stranger in every sense, and in the Maharajah he found a friend who always sought to attain "the secret understanding of the heart."[25] Mixed with this satisfaction was nevertheless a tinge of disappointment at his inability to accomplish anything concrete there—one of Forster's letters to his mother expresses the conflict succinctly: "Yes, I love H. H. and he me, and I am glad to have had this extraordinary experience, but it has been disappointing to be given so little that I can do and so much that I cannot."[26] This was written in late July of 1921, only a few days before the beginning of an elaborate festival marking the birth of Krishna. Forster's experience at this joyful and chaotic celebration proved a revelation, illuminating for him the notion that religious devotion can bring harmony to disparate human beings.

Forster and Hinduism: The Gokul Ashtami Festival

Forster's note in the Everyman edition of his novel emphasizes the powerful impact of the festival he attended in Dewas:

> The Krishna festival closely follows the great celebration of Gokul Ashtami, which I attended for nine days in the palace of Dewas State Senior, and which was the strangest and strongest Indian experience ever granted me.[27]

The festival Forster witnessed, also known as Janamastami,[28] is celebrated by Hindus throughout India, varying greatly from place to place in accordance with local tradition. Because Dewas was a Maratha state, the festival Forster observed there was heavily infused with elements of Maratha history and culture. An example of this is the chanting of the name of Tukaram, the great poet-saint of the region (" 'Tukaram, Tukaram, thou art my father and my mother and all things' we would sing, time after time, until we seemed to be worshipping a poet."),[29] which recurs at the beginning of the novel's third section as the song of Professor Godbole.[30] The invitation from the Maharajah was a great honor for Forster, as foreigners were rarely permitted to witness this most important event.

Many details from Forster's account of Gokul Ashtami have been transplanted intact into the novel—the single prisoner released from jail in honor of the holy day is one instance,[31] and another is the exuberant game involving butter and rice pudding played to amuse the newly born god.[32] Several critics (particularly June Perry Levine)[33] have noted the relationship between the author's Dewas experiences and the festival in the novel, but they have chosen not to discuss the nature of the transformation from life to art. In the final ceremony of the festival, a clay model of Krishna's birthplace (the village of Gokul, near Mathura) is immersed in the water amidst loud and prolonged celebration. Forster's account of this in *The Hill of Devi* is forthright and unadorned:

> By ten we reached the Tank and the queer impressive ceremony of drowning the Town of Gokul was performed. The town— about a yard square—was stripped of its flagstaffs, and, after prayers and meals, was handed to a man whose hereditary duty it is to drown the Town of Gokul. He was half naked and waded into the water and the darkness, pushing the city before him on a floating tray. When he was far out he upset it, all the dolls fell into the water and were seen no more, and the town, being of mud, dissolved immediately. The tray was brought back and worshipped slightly, while elephants trumpeted and cannon were fired.[34]

In the novel, however, the scene is monstrously inflated and infused with a sense of drama missing in the original:

> Suddenly . . . . the palanquin of Krishna appeared from behind a ruined wall, and descended the carven glistening watersteps. On either side of it, the singers tumbled, a woman prominent, a wild and beautiful young saint with flowers in her hair. She was praising God without attributes—thus did she apprehend Him. Others praised Him with attributes, seeing Him in this or that organ of the body or manifestation of the sky. Down they rushed to the foreshore and stood in the small waves, and a sacred meal was prepared, of which those who felt worthy partook. . . . Above stood the secular power of Mau—elephants, artillery, crowds—and high above them a wild tempest started, confined at first to the

upper regions of the air. Gusts of wind mixed darkness and light, sheets of rain cut from the north, stopped, cut from the south, began rising from below, and across them struggled the singers, sounding every note but terror, and preparing to throw God away, God Himself (not that God can be thrown), into the storm. . . .

The village of Gokul reappeared upon its tray. It was the substitute for the silver image, which never left its haze of flowers; on behalf of another symbol, it was to perish. A servitor took it in his hands, and tore off the blue and white streamers. He was naked, broad-shouldered, thin-waisted—the Indian body again triumphant—and it was his heredity office to close the gates of salvation. He entered the dark waters, pushing the village before him, until the clay dolls slipped off their chairs and began to gutter in the rain. . . .[35]

Here Forster has not only added descriptive details like the image of the wild female devotee, but has even enlisted the heavens themselves to provide a timely and suitably dramatic storm. The scene goes on, of course, to describe the capsizing of the boats, a mock-baptism in which Indians and English alike are immersed and rendered, for one ironic moment, entirely equal. Another dash of divine stage-noise gives the scene its final touch: "Artillery was fired, drums beaten, the elephants trumpeted and drowning all an immense peal of thunder, unaccompanied by lightning, cracked like a mallet on the dome."[36] Again Forster has taken personal experience as a basic outline, at the same time painting a vast backdrop against which he dramatizes the insignificance of individual human beings.

The principal mode of the Gokul Ashtami festival is confusion, yet Forster seems to feel that order has no definite value in this context: in his novel, he characterizes the disorder of the festival as "benign confusion."[37] This Hindu celebration is based upon incorporation: the contradictory components of reality are all embraced joyfully, for sweepers and criminals are included as well as princes. In this sense, Forster deliberately offers the festival in the novel as an answer to the echo of the caves, which "calls out for renunciation rather than incorporation."[38] Indeed, the entire final section of the book responds to the message of the caves ("Everything exists, nothing has value")[39] by presenting the latitudinarian mysticism of Professor Godbole and its own message, that of universal love:

> They loved all men, the whole universe, and scraps of their past, tiny splinters of detail, emerged for a moment to melt into the universal warmth. Thus Godbole, though she was not important to him, remembered an old woman he had met in Chandrapore days. Chance brought her into his mind while it was in this heated state, he did not select her, she happened to occur among the throng of soliciting images, a tiny splinter, and he impelled her by this spiritual force to that place where completeness can be found. Completeness, not reconstruction. His senses grew thinner, he remembered a wasp seen he forgot where, perhaps on a stone. He loved the wasp equally, he impelled it likewise, he was imitating God.[40]

Here Mrs. Moore, the bearer of the bleak and dispiriting echo, has returned in an affirmative role: her utter insignificance in Godbole's life only highlights the power of Hinduism to absorb and give meaning to all people and all things, as does the inclusion of the wasp.

In the world of Forster's novel, Hindu inclusivity is sharply contrasted with Christian exclusivity, as expressed in the famous scene where two Anglican missionaries discuss the limits of God's grace:

> In our Father's house are many mansions, they taught, and there alone will the incompatible multitudes of mankind be welcomed and soothed. Not one shall be turned away by the servants on that veranda, be he black or white, not one shall be kept standing who approaches with a loving heart. And why should the divine hospitality cease here? Consider, with all reverence, the monkeys. May there not be a mansion for the monkeys also? Old Mr. Graysford said No, but young Mr. Sorley, who was advanced, said Yes; he saw no reason why monkeys should not have their collateral share of bliss, and he had sympathetic discussions about them with his Hindu friends. And the jackals? Jackals were indeed less to Mr. Sorley's mind, but he admitted that the mercy of God, being infinite, may well embrace all mammals. And the wasps? He became uneasy during the descent to wasps, and was apt to change the conversation. And oranges, cactuses, crystals, and mud? and the bacteria inside Mr. Sorley? No, no, this is going too far. We must

exclude someone from our gathering, or we shall be left with nothing.[41]

Forster thus characterizes Christianity in the same manner that
he does Anglo-Indians: their world too is founded on the exclusion of everything incomprehensible or unfamiliar, and this for-
mula simply will not do in a land as protean and impenetrable
as India. If one thinks of India, with all its divisions
(Hindu/Muslim, Brahman/Untouchable, English/Indian) as a
metaphor for human existence, then Hinduism in Forster's
novel offers not an answer, but rather an illumination of sorts to
the crisis of personal relations that is taking place in the book.
Only Hinduism even begins to come to terms with the amorphous and intangible aspects of existence, and "poor little talk-
ative Christianity,"[42] as Mrs. Moore thinks of it, comes off badly
by comparison. The image of Christianity in *A Passage to India*
is a negative one because Forster considers this religion too self-
important: the author is speaking for himself when he asks
about Adela Quested, "Her particular brand of opinions, and the
suburban Jehovah who sanctified them—by what right did they
claim so much importance in the world, and assume the title of
civilization?"[43] But his fundamental objection to Christianity is
on humanistic grounds—he simply feels no warmth for Christ
the man and suspects that this coolness is mutual. Forster artic-
ulated this viewpoint most lucidly in an address to the Cambridge Humanists in 1959:

> The Christ we know is what the gospels tell us he was, we cannot
> see behind them or discount the misrepresentations they may con-
> tain and even in the Gospels there is much that Christ says and
> does that I do like and often think about—the parable of the hid-
> den talent, for instance. . . . And I am touched by the birth
> stories, and overwhelmed by the death story. But there is so much
> on the other side, so much moving away from worldliness towards
> preaching and threats, so much emphasis on followers, on an elite,
> so little intellectual power . . . , such an absence of humour and
> fun that my blood's chilled. I would on the whole rather not meet
> the speaker, either at an Eliot cocktail party or for a quick quaker
> talk, and the fact that my rejection is not vehement does not save
> it from being tenacious. It may seem absurd to turn from Christ to

Krishna, that vulgar blue-faced boy with his romps and butter-pats: Krishna is usually a trivial figure. But he does admit pleasure and fun and their connection with love.[44]

Love and fun are of course both central in the Gokul Ashtami festival: Forster's account in the novel of the general merriment again makes an explicit comparison with Christianity:

"God si love!" There is fun in heaven. God can play practical jokes upon Himself, draw chairs away from beneath His own posteriors, set His own turbans on fire, and steal His own petticoats when He bathes. By sacrificing good taste, this worship achieved what Christianity has shirked: the inclusion of merriment. All spirit as well as all matter must participate in salvation, and if practical jokes are banned, the circle is incomplete.[45]

Forster rejects Christianity because it offers in Christ a figure who has too little to do with love, or even friendship:

. . . I don't desire to meet Christ personally, and, since personal relations mean everything to me, this has helped me to cool off from Christianity. If the religion of my fathers (i.e. C. of E.) had provided me with a more satisfactory father-figure, brother-figure, friend, what you will, I might have been more tempted to stay in it. It contained much that I respected and respect, but too little that I could care for.[46]

One element of the festival at Dewas that Forster found moving was the mystical devotionalism of the Maharajah. In Forster's eyes, those who had heeded the promptings of the divine were set apart from other men, they were somehow finer in spirit. He offers his view on mysticism in an unpublished essay on Kipling:

Kim is Kipling. It is the one book that we must bear in mind when we are trying to estimate his genius, for it contains the spiritual standards by which all his developments must be measured. Mysticism may be a mistake, but no one will deny this—that if once a man shows traces of it, those traces must be carefully scanned by all who are trying to understand him. To have felt, if only for a moment, that this visible world is an illusion—to have conceived, however faintly, that the real is the unseen, to have had a passing desire for the One—is at once to be marked off from all those who have not thus felt, thus conceived, thus denied. There is no explanation of the gift of mysticism, many criminals and out-casts have possessed it; many bishops, if the truth were known, are devoid of it, it pays no honour to rank, character, or avocation; only one thing is certain; it is the particular gift of India, and India has given it to Kipling, as she gave it to his boy here, Kim.[47]

In the Maharajah's sincere and unwavering search for union with the divine, Forster found an intensity of religious feeling previously unknown to him. The final comments in *The Hill of Devi* stress the ruler's spiritual quest and his all-embracing notion of divinity:

> His religion was the deepest thing in him. It ought to be studied—neither by the psychologist nor by the mythologist but by the individual who has 'experienced similar promptings. He penetrated into rare regions and he was always hoping that others would follow him there. He was never exclusive, despite his endless pujahs. To recall the conversation that we had forty years ago in an upper room at Delhi, he was hopeful that we should all be recalled to the attention of God.[48]

The authenticity of the Maharajah's religious beliefs prompted Forster to shed his instinctive skepticism about religion and enabled him to appreciate those aspects of Hinduism which nourished humanistic values.

It is a mistake, however, to infer that Forster's attraction to Hindu concepts of universal love indicates an uncritical acceptance of Hinduism. Just as Ralph and Stella Moore "like Hinduism, though they take no interest in its forms,"[49] Forster finds Hindu ritual, with its profusion of decorative objects and endless ceremonies, generally unappealing. The trappings of Hinduism disturbed his fastidious aestheticism, but he was too much the humanist to pass judgment when he saw the effect on the worshipers. In a letter to his mother, he described the Gokul Ashtami's lack of decorum:

> What troubles me is that every detail, almost without exception, is fatuous and in bad taste. The altar is a mass of little objects, stifled with rose leaves, the walls are hung with deplorable oleographs, the chandeliers, draperies—everything bad. Only one thing is beautiful—the expression on the faces of the people as they bow to the shrine. . . .[50]

Forster's essay on Hindu temple architecture emphasizes the same dichotomy between form and meaning:

> the general deportment of the Temple is odious. It is unaccommodating, it rejects every human grace, its jokes are ill-bred, its fair ladies are fat, it ministers neither to the sense of beauty nor to the sense of time, and it is discontented with its own material. No one could love such a building. Yet no one could forget it. It remains in the mind when fairer types have faded, and sometimes seems to be the only type that has any significance.[51]

Unlike G. L. Dickinson, who was overcome by his aesthetic distaste for Hindu art, Forster was able to learn from Hinduism despite his dislike for its formal manifestations. His openness to all aspects of life at Dewas in 1921 made him a popular figure who was often complemented for his interest in Indian customs. After sitting for hours at a religious ceremony with an aching back, Forster was approached by an Indian who told him, "We are pained to see your pain . . . but we are greatly pleased by your so good nature. We have not met an Englishman like you previously."[52] One man who remembers Forster's Dewas days gives the following account of his popularity:

> The people who met Forster and saw him when he was in Dewas State Service said that he was very sociable and kind to them. They liked him because he mixed freely amongst them and took much interest in their religious revelations; also because he used to put on Indian dress, which he enjoyed. . . . Whenever he walked in the town or appeared at functions, they used to cheer him. For them, he was a surprising person because very few foreigners who visited Dewas had any interest in talking to them or meeting them.[53]

Forster came to view his six months at Dewas as a success: he had been offered a rare and intimate glimpse of Indian life, and the affection he freely proffered was returned in the same spirit. With its creative, life-affirming chaos, the Gokul Ashtami festival deepened his understanding of Hinduism and gave him the inspiration needed for the final section of his novel.

Visits with Syed Ross Masood

Within a fortnight of Forster's arrival at Dewas in 1921, Syed Ross Masood arrived from Hyderabad, where he was now Director of Public Instruction. Although the two had corresponded steadily throughout the years, this was their first meeting since Forster's 1912–13 journey to India. In his delight at this reunion, Forster initially failed to recognize that two entirely different worlds were meeting for the first time here:

> I had not realised when [Masood] came to see me at Dewas how dramatic the occasion was. Two extremes were meeting. He had never stayed at a Maratha court before, and the Marathas had never coped with such a guest. There was some nervousness on both sides. On Masood's it took the form of incisiveness and pomposity. He held forth rather too emphatically on the power and wealth of His Exalted Highness the Nizam of Hyderabad and his salute of twenty-one guns. (We had only fifteen.) Willowy and deferential, Malarao listened to him, making polite sounds. H. H. was also extremely courteous, and behaved almost as to a fellow ruler: there were certain civilities and attentions which Masood had not expected to receive and they gratified him. . . . After three days of Hinduism, Masood retired with his clerks and his files to Hyderabad. Our incompetence distressed him more than it could me because he saw it as an extreme example of his country's inefficiency.[54]

This meeting of two proud Indian traditions, one Hindu and one Muslim, was fraught with possibilities for conflict, but as Forster notes in a letter to Malcolm Darling, both parties rose to the occasion and behaved with great politeness:

> Masood is here, having speeded from Hyderabad, and very funny it has been to watch the contest between his heavy premier Moslem artillery and the light Maratha bowman, a contest that is conducted with high courtesy on both sides, and I think with mutual respect.[55]

Forster later returned Masood's visit, coming to Hyderabad in July, and again for several weeks in November, when he had finished his stay in Dewas. With its urbane atmosphere and beautiful scenery, Hyderabad was a relief for Forster after six genial but confining months in Dewas.[56] A letter home echoes the delight he had felt upon first seeing Hyderabad in 1913:

> I am having a lovely time here and enjoy every moment of it. Masood in such good form, the weather perfect and exhilarating, beautiful things to look at, interesting people to talk to, delicious food, romantic walks, pretty birds in the garden. . . .[57]

After several days in Hyderabad during which he also visited an old friend from 1913 (Sir M. A. Hydari), Forster was taken along by Masood on the latter's inspection tour of primary schools in the western portion of the state. While Masood worked, Forster spent most of his time sightseeing: at the tomb of Ali Barid in Bidar, he saw an inscription which reappears in *A Passage to India:*

> Alas, without me for thousands of years
> The Rose will blossom and the Spring will bloom,
> But those who have secretly understood my heart—
> They will approach and visit the grave where I lie.[58]

This poem occupies Aziz's thoughts in the instant before he meets Mrs. Moore in the mosque and it foreshadows the enduring bond between these two unlikely friends:

> He had seen the quatrain on the tomb of a Deccan king and regarded it as profound philosophy—he always held pathos to be profound. The secret understanding of the heart! He repeated the phrase with tears in his eyes, and as he did so one of the pillars in the mosque seemed to quiver. It swayed in the gloom and detached itself. Belief in ghosts ran in his blood, but he sat firm. Another pillar moved, a third, and then an Englishwoman stepped out into the moonlight.[59]

Accompanying Forster and Masood on this tour was Syed Ali Akbar, the Divisional Inspector of Schools for the region. In an article written in 1970, he offers another glimpse of Forster at Bidar:

> During the three days of our stay at Bidar, while Forster was engaged in sightseeing, Masood and I had a busy time inspecting the local schools. Forster had an illustrated book of Indian birds

with him. He would get up early in the morning while Masood and I were still asleep and go out into the country with the book to watch the birds. His joy knew no bounds when he succeeded in identifying a bird.[60]

This enthusiasm for bird-watching probably explains the frequent and knowledgeable references to Indian birds in his novel.

Syed Ali Akbar also records an incident which bears a remarkable resemblance to a significant part of the scene at the Marabar Caves:

> The following day we left for Gungawati, en route to Hampi. On our way we sighted the Mudgal fort situated on the top of a hill. Mudgal was not included in our programme, but we had to halt there because Forster insisted on visiting the fort. A police inspector approached us and conducted us to the primary school nearby. We asked him the way up to the fort. He said that the path to it was dangerous, entirely blocked by cactus hedge. We did our best to dissuade Forster from carrying out his intention, but he was adamant and boldly declared, "I will take the risk." Getting annoyed, Masood said, "Morgan, you are impossible. You may go but Akbar and I are not coming. We are going to inspect the primary school here." Forster had hardly left with the police inspector and a couple of villagers for twenty minutes when he came back to the primary school covered with cactus thorns. He was in agony. The police inspector informed us that there was a good doctor at Gungawati. We proceeded there in the evening and it took three days for Forster to recover completely.[61]

This seems a clear instance of personal experience transformed directly into fiction: after the incident in the caves, Adela Quested rushed down a hill covered with cactuses, and later "hundreds of cactus spines had to be picked out of her flesh."[62] Forster's description of Adela's treatment ("Hour after hour Miss Derek and Mrs. McBryde examined her through magnifying glasses, always coming on fresh colonies, tiny hairs that might snap off and be drawn into the blood if they were neglected")[63] is most likely derived from painful personal memories.

When *A Passage to India* appeared in 1924, the dedication

read, "To Syed Ross Masood and to the seventeen years of our friendship," [64] an obvious indication of Masood's crucial role in shaping Forster's vision of India. The novel had as its principal Indian character a young Muslim who resembled Masood in many ways. Accounts of Masood's personality from those who were close to him all stress characteristics which describe Aziz equally well. The foremost of these is a passion for Urdu and Persian poetry: Aziz is always quoting poetry to his friends and his daydreams are frequently flavored with delicate and melancholic verses lamenting the sad state of contemporary Islam. In the very first scene in which he appears, Aziz recites poetry to his companions as they wait for dinner:

> Presently . . . Aziz began quoting poetry, Persian, Urdu, a little Arabic. His memory was good, and for so young a man he had read largely; the themes he preferred were the decay of Islam and the brevity of love. They listened delighted, for they took the public view of poetry, not the private which obtains in England. It never bored them to hear words, words; they breathed them with the cool night air, never stopping to analyse; the name of the poet, Hafiz, Hali, Iqbal, was sufficient guarantee. [65]

K. G. Saiyidain recalls Masood's constant recourse to the same poets in similar social settings:

> He had a passionate fondness for poetry and knew thousands of lines in different languages by heart. His favourite poets in Urdu were Meer, Anis, Hali, and Iqbal, and he would recite the greater part of their poetical works without any hesitation.
>
> For Persian he had a passionate fondness and he had a charming way of reciting from great Persian poets whenever the company was congenial. [66]

Hand in hand with this love of poetry went a great flamboyance, a dramatic and arresting physical presence that nearly everyone who knew Masood commented upon. H. C. Dhanda, who worked with Masood in the Muslim state of Bhopal in the 1930s, calls him "one of the most stimulating and lovable personalities I ever knew: he was in every way uplifting company." [67] K. G. Saiyidain remembers a certain theatricality about Masood:

Chesterton has somewhere said that exaggeration is the definition of art. He knew how to utilize the art of exaggeration in his speech so as to produce the maximum effect in telling an anecdote or drawing a word-picture of a scene or character. But there was no malice or desire to offend in this exaggeration. It was just an artistic device, employed in the spirit of an artist.[68]

Aziz at Fielding's garden party is pure Masood: utterly charming, very much the center of attention, and given to picturesque exaggerations (in this case, the Mughal emperors' imaginary underground water system) which even the doggedly honest Fielding is too entertained to refute.

Both Masood and Aziz are "Islamic modernists" who support the removal of purdah, and Aziz's facetious and casual comment to Fielding on British rule ("When I was a student I got excited over your damned countrymen, certainly; but if they'll let me get on with my profession and not be too rude to me officially, I really don't ask for more")[69] in an adaption of Masood's favorite pronouncement on the subject: "As for your damned countrymen, I pity the poor fellows from the bottom of my heart, and give them all the help I can."[70] Aziz later comes to regret this light-hearted attitude, telling Hamidullah after his trial, "My great mistake has been taking our rulers as a joke,"[71] but Masood, even while engaged in acrimonious debate with British officials, never lost his good humor about the follies of the Ruling Race. All of these details clearly indicate that Masood was the model for the volatile young doctor: in Aziz, Forster has created a loving but honest portrait of his closest Indian friend which lends a vital energy to the novel.[72]

chapter 6

Return to India: 1945

The Years 1922–45

Forster's 1921 visit gave him the impetus needed to finish the Indian novel he had begun in 1913. Anticipating that the second journey might restimulate his creativity, he had brought with him the pages already written, but India proved too overwhelming, too immediate:

> When I returned in 1921 to stay with the Maharajah I took the chapters with me and expected that the congenial surroundings would inspire me to go on. Exactly the reverse happened. Between the India I had tried to create and the India I was experiencing there was an impassable gulf. I had to get back to England and see my material in perspective before I could proceed. Perhaps the long wait was to the good and the religious atmosphere of Dewas certainly helped to establish the spiritual sequence I was seeking, particularly in the last section of the book.[1]

The rigors of an Indian hot season, so vividly described in *The Hill of Devi,* offer another explanation for Forster's inability to continue his novel in Dewas. On his arrival back in England at the beginning of 1922, his concentration returned, and the years 1922 and 1923 were mostly taken up with the writing of *A Passage to India.* By early 1924 Forster had finished his novel, but he was doubtful of its value; only the steadfast reassurances of Leonard Woolf convinced him that it was worthy of publication.[2] Caught up in the excitement attending the final arrangements for the novel's publication, Forster soon shed the depression which so many writers experience upon completing a major work. Writing later to Bessie Trevelyan (Bob Trevelyan's wife), he was far more happy:

> It was very good of you to write and tell me you were enjoying the book. Your letter cheered me a good deal, for I was in the mood for thinking the book bad. Since I heard from you others have praised it also and I am happier. Perhaps it will have a topical success anyway, but that depends on whether those who dislike it can also get through it. . . . The Anglo-Indian is not exaggerated in the least. He is like that only worse. Ask Bob or Goldie.[3]

This letter's rather defensive closing is undoubtedly Forster's response to criticisms of *A Passage to India* which had appeared in both India and England. Numerous Anglo-Indians, many of them retired Indian civil servants who viewed the past through a romantic haze, sprang to attack the novel for its unflattering portrayal of the English community of Chandrapore. E. A. Horne's letter in the *New Statesman* was one of the most vehement expressions of dismay at Forster's Anglo-Indian characters:

> But the Anglo-Indians? Where have they come from? What planet do they inhabit? One rubs one's eyes. They are not even good caricatures, for an artist must see his original clearly before he can successfully caricature it. They are puppets, simulacra.[4]

Horne goes on to castigate Forster for his failure to see "the real Anglo-India" and ends by parodying Fielding's advice to Adela Quested on how to see "the real India" (i.e., "Try seeing Indians"):

> Why are these people and these incidents so wildly improbable and unreal? The explanation is a singular but a simple one. Mr. Forster went out to India to see, and to study, and to make friends of Indians. He did not go out to India to see Anglo-Indians: and most of what he knows of them, their ways and their catchwords, and has put into his book, he has picked up from the stale gossip of Indians, just as the average Englishman who goes out to India picks up most of what he knows about Indians from other Englishmen. It is a curious revenge that the Indian enjoys in the pages of Mr. Forster's novel which profess to deal with Anglo-Indian life and manners; and some would say a just one. All the same, it is a thousand pities that Mr. Forster did not see the real Anglo-India,

for he would have written an incomparably better and truer book; and we venture to suggest to him, next time he goes to India: "Try seeing Anglo-Indians."[5]

That such controversy would arise is not surprising, for Forster's relentless honesty in depicting Anglo-Indians as he perceived them was the antithesis of traditional Anglo-Indian fiction, which constantly glossed over the shortcomings of the rulers while emphasizing the inherent flaws of the ruled. The impulse to glorify the guardians of Empire at the expense of Indians is apparent in a response to Forster's novel by Yvonne Fitzroy, who was in 1924 private secretary to Lady Reading, the wife of the Viceroy:

> A little more than a year ago *The Passage to India* [sic] descended on the dovecotes of Simla. I have never visited the depressing station of Mr. Forster's inspiration, and in the picture drawn of the social relations between the two races, I must confess to having found it remote from my own experience. That the types portrayed exist among Englishmen and women is of course true, but the book suggests the general rather than the particular, and such an attitude of bored and indifferent condescension did not seem to me general. For all that, it must be admitted that there are many instances of British discourtesy to the Indian which have made of warm friends bitter enemies; no question of studied insult, but purely self-absorption and lack of consideration. I have been told that in this respect women are the worst offenders. On the other hand, the Indian is ultra-sensitive . . . and he is also a trifle vain![6]

This represents a common Anglo-Indian attitude about social relations: "perhaps there's been a bit of rudeness, yes, but after all, Indians are so extraordinarily touchy." In this way, many discussions of the failings of the English in India came around inevitably to what was wrong with Indians.

For many English readers, however, *A Passage to India* was a startling and effective indictment of the Raj, and it prompted them finally to decide that benevolent paternal rule no longer had a future in India. Those icons which Kipling and Mrs. Steel had so lovingly erected were shattered by an author appealing to the postwar English cynicism and disillusionment with prevailing values. The traditional Anglo-Indian novel, with its wicked Brahman priests and tragic interracial liaisons, had scant credibility after 1924: having read Forster's novel, readers were no longer willing to put up with the one-dimensional "natives" who were a standard feature of most Anglo-Indian fiction.

On the Indian side, A Passage to India was likewise credited with "humanizing" Indian characters; Forster's portrayal of them as complex and fully developed personalities was a welcome change. One Indian described his feelings in an article which appeared in Nation and Athenaeum in 1928:

> When I read A Passage to India, I was filled with a sense of great relief and of an almost personal gratitude to Mr. Forster. This was not because as an Indian I felt myself vindicated or flattered by the book. Indeed to know oneself is not to feel flattered, as many an Anglo-Indian reader of the book has discovered before me. It was because for the first time I saw myself reflected in the mind of an English author, without losing all semblance of a human face. . . . Mr. Forster in A Passage to India has created the Easterner in English literature, for he is the first to raise grotesque legendary creatures and terracotta figures to the dignity of human beings.[7]

Most Indian reviewers echoed these sentiments, and the ensuing years have hardly diminished the great regard in which the book is held in India.

A frequent criticism of the novel from those who knew India well was that it was outdated, particularly in the portrayal of race relations:

> Even about the general background, however, there is a slight air of unreality. This is partly because the picture is out of date. The period is obviously before the War. Not that this matters, provided it is clearly understood. It is not only that the Lieutenant-Governor and dogcarts are out of date. All the fuss about the "bridge" party will strike the Anglo-Indian reader as hopelessly out of date, it being nowadays very much the fashion—not in Delhi and Simla only, but in the humble mofussil station also—to entertain and cultivate Indians of good social standing.[8]

Despite the unmistakable note of snobbery in the last sentence, this is in many respects a just complaint, for Forster's conception of the state of human relations in India is derived almost solely from his first journey. K. Natwar-Singh has rightly pointed out the puzzlement of many readers which was caused by the "broken chronology" of the novel:

> Forster would have been spared a great deal of criticism if more people . . . had read Rose Macaulay's comment, "some confusion is perhaps caused by the book's doubtful chronology, for it deals with the India of one period, is written largely from material collected and from a point of view derived from that period, and was published twelve years later, when Indians and English had got into quite another state." The "doubtful chronology" of the book did indeed create confusion.
> It depicts a pre-1914 India, and by the time it was published in 1924 events had overtaken it. It appears to be an almost anti-national book since it makes no mention of the political ferment that was going on in India in the early twenties.[9]

The portions of the novel written after 1921 are pervaded by Forster's awareness of a new era. It is now too late for sympathy and understanding: only when India is free will there be a basis for social relationships. This is the ultimate meaning of the final scene in the book, where the phrase "No, not yet"[10] points with tentative hope to a future when Aziz and Fielding can meet as equals. In a letter from Hyderabad at the end of his 1921 visit, Forster calmly expressed his conviction that improvements in English manners could no longer satisfy Indian aspirations:

> I have been with pro-Government and pro-English Indians all the time, so cannot realise the feeling of the other party: and am only sure of this—that we were paying for the insolence of Englishmen and Englishwomen out here in the past. I don't mean that good manners can avert a political upheaval. But they can minimise it, and come nearer to averting it in the East than elsewhere. English manners out here have improved wonderfully in the last eight years. Some people are frightened, others seem really to have undergone a change of heart.
> But it's too late. Indians don't long for social intercourse with Englishmen any longer. They have made a life of their own.[11]

This final realization lies at the heart of all interracial relationships portrayed in A Passage to India and inspires the au-

thor's vision of future possibilities for social relations. Forster's
failure to present in his novel the great nationalist movement
sweeping India in the 1920s is a reflection of the book's clear origins in the earlier, prewar period, but it is also a measure of the
author's scrupulous honesty. As he admitted in his letter from
Hyderabad, he simply hadn't met any nationalists and therefore
lacked the direct experience necessary to bring them to life as
fictional characters. Forster's familiarity with the nationalist
movement is indicated by two articles he wrote for *Nation and
Athenaeum* in 1922 under the heading "Reflections in India."
The first is subtitled "Too Late?" and contains an incisive analy-
sis of India's new political consciousness, while the second
("The Prince's Progress") attacks the visit to India of the Prince
of Wales in detailed and forthright terms, warning that the vigor
of the freedom struggle will not fade.[12] A third article by Forster
from 1922 entitled "India and the Turk" traces the origins of the
Khilafat movement to his old acquaintances the Ali brothers and
exhibits his emotional and political grasp of an issue close to the
hearts of Indian Muslims.[13]

In the years after the publication of *A Passage to India* in
1924, Forster turned increasingly toward social criticism, be-
coming an eloquent spokesman for individual liberties. Ironically, these activities brought him a measure of fame that had
eluded him as a novelist; his frequent radio broadcasts, book
reviews, and feature articles kept him constantly in the public
eye. Laurence Brander considers Forster's work in the thirties
his most influential:

> As the twenties faded into the haunted thirties, in that nightmare
> decade Forster became the embodiment of the liberal man of let-
> ters, precociously a grand old man, because he was free and ready
> to take up good causes, to speak and write for freedom of expres-
> sion. This was his greatest decade as a social influence: in a dec-
> ade of Leaders, he led our young writers, a humanist in a world of
> idealist communists and High Churchmen.[14]

Forster had scant contact with India in this period, with the
exception of several welcome visits from Syed Ross Masood,
who came to Europe in the 1930s to see both Forster and Sir

Theodore Morison, his former guardian, who then lived in Paris. Masood's widow Amtul (now Begum Chhatari) recalls gay visits to Forster in England during which her initial awe of her husband's old friend was soon melted by his casual charm.[15] Masood's death in 1937 greatly saddened Forster, who contributed a warm remembrance of his friend to a memorial number of the journal *Urdu*.[16] Another melancholy task for Forster was his obituary in the *Times* of the Maharajah of Dewas, who died in disgrace and exile at Pondicherry only five months after Masood.[17]

Throughout the thirties and forties, Forster gave monthly broadcasts on the BBC Eastern Service under the title "We Speak to India: Some Books,"[18] These programs consisted of his lively and inevitably charitable comments on current books of interest to his Indian listening audience. In a broadcast after the outbreak of the Second World War, Forster affirmed the enduring relevance for him of Hinduism's emphasis on individual spiritual quest. Speaking to India from a war-torn London, he describes his reaction to a photographic exhibit on Hindu art:

> I came away feeling not only that Hindu art is a remarkable achievement—that I had always realised—but that it was an achievement which I might interpret in view of my own experiences and needs.
>
> For you cannot imagine how much we over here are in need of inspiration, of spirituality, of something which will deliver us from the tyranny of the body-politic. Besides our war versus totalitarianism, we have also an inner war, a struggle for truer values, a struggle of the individual towards the dark secret place where he may find reality. I came away thinking "Yes, the people who built these temples, the people who planned Khajraho and Orissa and Madura—knew about that. They belonged to another civilization, but they knew . . . that the community cannot satisfy the human spirit."[19]

These widely admired broadcasts helped maintain the links between Indian and English intellectuals during the war, and they also paved the way for Forster's final visit to India in 1945. In his novel *Down There on a Visit*, Christopher Isherwood sums up Forster's importance in this period as a symbol of humanistic values. Isherwood describes Forster as

> the antiheroic hero, with his straggly straw mustache, his light, gay blue baby eyes and his elderly stoop. Instead of a folded umbrella or a brown uniform, his emblems are his tweed cap (which is too small for him) and the odd-shaped brown paper parcels in which he carries his belongings from country to town and back again. While the others tell their followers to be ready to die, he advises us to live as if we were immortal. And he really does this himself, although he is anxious and afraid as any of us, and never for an instant pretends not to be. He and his books and what they stand for are all that is truly worth saving from Hitler. . . . [20]

Final Passage: 1945

Forster's final passage to India in 1945 was made possible by an invitation from the all-India PEN[21] Club (actually a chapter of the International PEN), a writers' organization devoted to bringing together India's diverse languages and literary traditions. In recognition of his long commitment to Indian culture, Forster was asked to address the PEN conference at Jaipur in November 1945. This last visit began very differently from the first two, when he had followed the traditional sea route to India via Suez—this time he arrived by air, getting his first look at India from above:

> It was a dull, cold Friday morning in October 1945 when I left England. Two days later, on the Sunday afternoon, I was in India. Below me lay the desert of Rajputana, baked by the sun and blotched with the shadows of clouds. The plane came down for half an hour near the dragon-shaped fort of Jodhpur, then took off again, and it was Delhi. I felt dazed. And we had travelled so fast that we were ahead of schedule, and had no one to meet us.[22]

But the shock of this abrupt arrival could not dampen his enthusiasm at being back in India; his initial fascination was not unlike that he had felt in 1912:

Suddenly very slow, instead of very quick, we jogged in a tonga through the Delhi bazaars, our luggage in front, our legs hanging down behind, the dust rising, the sun setting, the smoke drifting out of the little shops. It became dark and the sky was covered with stars. Were we lost? No. An unknown host, an Indian, received us, and next day I stood on the high platform of the Great Mosque, one of the noblest buildings in India and the world. Profound thankfulness filled me. The sky was now intensely blue, the kites circled round and round the pearl-grey domes and the red frontispiece of sandstone, sounds drifted up from Delhi city, the pavement struck warm through the soles of my socks; I was back in the country I loved, after an absence of twenty-five years.[23]

Although in his late sixties, Forster was still an energetic and ambitious tourist, re-visiting Delhi, Bombay, Jaipur, and Hyderabad, and seeing Bikaner and Calcutta for the first time— all in little more than a month. His host in Delhi and companion for the first several weeks was Ahmed Ali, who had met Forster in England in 1939. Forster's visit to India six years later cemented the friendship: Ahmed Ali was perhaps Forster's closest Indian friend in his later years. In a passage from "India Again" which echoes the atmosphere of the novel and also recalls his first journey, Forster notes the changelessness of the Indian countryside:

Externally the place has not changed. It looks much as it did from the train. Outside the carriage windows (the rather dirty windows) it unrolls as before—monotonous, enigmatic, and at moments sinister. And in some long motor drives which I took through the Deccan there were the same combinations of hill, rock, bushes, ruins, dusty people and occasional yellow flowers which I encountered when I walked on the soil in my youth.[24]

Yet two very important changes struck Forster at once: the increased political awareness of Indians, and the considerable change in the status of Indian women. He looked upon the first with wariness, for it aroused his innate suspicion of those who subordinate art to politics:

The big change I noticed was the increased interest in politics. You cannot understand the modern Indians unless you realise that politics occupy them passionately and constantly, that artistic problems . . . are subsidiary. Their attitude is "first we must find the correct political solution, and then we can deal with other matters." I think the attitude unsound, and used to say so; still, there it is, and they hold it much more vehemently than they did a quarter of a century ago. When I spoke about the necessity of form in literature and the importance of the individual vision, their attention wandered, although they listened politely. Literature, in their view, should expound or inspire a political creed.[25]

The second transformation was more to Forster's liking, and he noted its far-reaching consequences for India's future:

> It is when you leave the country, or the streets of the town, and go into the private houses, that you begin to notice a second great alteration, second only to politics—namely, the lifting of purdah, the increasing emancipation of women. . . . I have been in my life three times to Hyderabad, some of my happiest Indian days were spent there, so I have been able to trace this change. My first visit was in 1912 and then I saw scarcely any Indian women. My second visit was in 1921, when I was admitted into some family circles and saw a good deal of what may be called "semi-purdah"— ladies coming out into company, but not coming avowedly, and retiring at any moment behind the veil if they felt disposed to do so. Today, purdah has broken down at Hyderabad, except amongst the most conservative, and at the receptions to which I went the women sometimes outnumbered the men. . . . I don't know how far into society this lifting of the veil has extended. But I imagine that sooner or later the change will extend to the villages and transform the Indian social fabric from top to bottom.[26]

Forster's comments on the various cities he visited in 1945 are sometimes frankly nostalgic. In a letter to his 1912 traveling companion Bob Trevelyan recalling their first morning in Bombay over thirty years ago, he seems happier with the city than he did then:

> Bombay is improved. . . . It is indeed delightful, a sort of Alexandria set in Plymouth Sound. I wonder where it was that we three landed in the boat, rowed by the more unsuccessful apostles, 33 years ago. Do you remember our landing?[27]

After several unhappy days in the turmoil of Calcutta, Forster proceeded to Hyderabad, where fond memories were revived by a warm welcome from his old companions, Sajjad and Ahmed Mirza:

> What a dreadful place Calcutta is, and how glad I was after a lonely and adventurous journey of two days to arrive at Hyderabad and find no less than five old friends (and their four new sons) on the platform to meet me. All was instant luxury and health. Exhilarating chaotic city much improved, and now one of the nicest in India.[28]

In Hyderabad he also visited the Hydari family and Masood's former school inspector Syed Ali Akbar, who took Forster on a picnic to the Golconda tombs.[29]

The rest of the journey was a pleasant jumble—a visit to Tagore's Shantiniketan, a chat with the prominent Bengali painter Jamini Roy (who gave Forster one of his pictures), and a dash through the Rajputana desert to see the fort at Bikaner were some of the highlights. Forster also sampled Indian cinema in Bombay, visited the new Osmania University at Hyderabad which Masood had helped to found, and of course spoke with many Indian writers, both at the Jaipur conference and elsewhere. In all, it was a varied and stimulating visit which allowed Forster enough time both to renew old acquaintances and to see something of the considerable changes since his last journey.

Not surprisingly, Forster's own evaluation of the experience stresses personal contact with Indians and reminds one of his comment on the 1921 journey that "my deepest wish was to be alone with them."[30] He overheard several "indignant colonels at Delhi" saying of him, "What next! Fancy sending out old gentlemen who fall ill and can do no possible good."[31] Forster's answer to this, a reaffirmation of the value of personal relations, constitutes his modest summation of this last visit to India: "Old I am, gentleman I may or may not be, ill I was not. I have never felt better. And did I do any good? Yes, I did. I wanted to be with Indians, and I was, and that is a very little step in the right direction."[32]

The Old Man at King's: 1945-70

After the death of his mother in 1945, Forster was unable to retain ownership of his beloved house at Abinger in Surrey. The problem of where to live was solved when King's College, Cambridge elected him an Honorary Fellow and then accorded him the rare additional privilege of residing there.[33] This offer from his old college was gratefully accepted, and Forster spent the last twenty-five years of his life most happily as King's unofficial resident man-of-letters.[34] As his reputation as an artist and humanist grew, a steady stream of visitors came to his door: it was common knowledge in Cambridge that he never turned anyone away. He was especially happy to meet visitors from India and in this way carefully maintained his close ties to that country.

When Indian independence came on August 15, 1947, Forster gave a broadcast on the BBC Eastern Service entitled "Message to India." It is a valuable illustration of his enduring individual outlook: though he gives a passing nod to the historical significance of the day, his emphasis is once again on the strong bonds of personal affection that have made India a special place for him. Recalling his two closest Indian friends, he sends a hopeful blessing for the future:

> Today, the country I have known as India enters the past and becomes part of history. A new period opens, and my various Indian friends are now citizens of the new India or of Pakistan. You must excuse me if I begin with my friends. They are much in my mind on this momentous occasion. It is nearly forty years since I met, here in England, the late Syed Ross Masood. But for Masood, I should never have come to your part of the world. And but for another friend, the late Maharajah of Dewas Senior, I might never have returned to it. I mention these two names to indicate my position. The tie that has bound me in the past is affection. And today, with the future dawning, I think with love of those who are gone, and I wish the beloved ones who remain happiness and strength and peace.[35]

Two more acquaintances from his Indian past were renewed in the same year when the young Maharajah of Dewas (son of

Forster's friend, and later Maharajah of Kolhapur) visited him in London, bringing with him Major Sardar Deolekr, who had been Forster's assistant at Dewas in 1921.[36] Noticing the strong resemblance between father and son, Forster later wrote that he found the young man "so like his father physically that I kept forgetting that a generation had passed and that I was addressing a stranger."[37]

Other men and women, all much younger than Forster, helped keep him in touch with his Indian days; one was the writer Santha Rama Rau, who wrote a dramatic version of *A Passage to India* which eventually appeared in London's West End and later on Broadway. Though Forster usually rejected requests for permission to adapt his novels to plays or films, he agreed to make an exception for this perfect stranger who had simply sent him the script of her play without any prior introduction. In a program note for the opening night of the play in 1960, Forster wrote:

> Miss Rau has given up her creative work in order to dramatise a novel written by a foreigner on the subject of her own country. If international generosity exists anywhere, it is here, it is here, and most warmly do I thank her.[38]

Forster's Indian friends from his later life all emphasize his humility and generosity. Ahmed Ali recalls Forster's tireless (and successful) efforts in 1940 to obtain a publisher for his novel *Twilight in Delhi,* which Forster later praised in a note to the Everyman edition of *A Passage to India:* "The civilization, or blend of civilizations, which produced Aziz has been movingly evoked by the novelist, Ahmed Ali, in his *Twilight in Delhi.*"[39] Other friends included Raja Rao and Mulk Raj Anand, whom Forster also aided in their struggle for recognition as young writers, and K. Natwar-Singh, who in 1964 edited a volume of personal appreciations entitled *E. M. Forster: A Tribute.* These men remained in close touch with Forster, who corresponded regularly with them throughout the 1960s despite his fragile health.[40]

Forster's assessment of the nuclear age was essentially pessimistic: he was instinctively suspicious of the claims of tech-

nology and felt that individuals were of increasingly less importance in modern society. Yet he never despaired, never lost his
faith in the power of personal relations to create islands of affection and order in a chaotic world. A letter from Forster to
Ahmed Ali in 1963 thanking him for his contribution to Natwar-
Singh's collection of tributes stubbornly restated his old belief in
human relations:

> My dear Ahmed
>   I am deeply moved by your contribution to the Tribute book. I
> have just read it and never expected anything would appear so on
> the spot and in the heart. You bring back so much to me and so
> lovingly. I read it too in such an affectionate place—the house of
> the Buckinghams, whom you mention. They live at Coventry now,
> and maintain my faith in human relationships—I don't, you know,
> admit that my view of human nature has been invalidated, though
> economical and political affairs are being led by science at an in-
> creasing rate towards disaster.[41]

This letter goes on to mention some common friends and ends
with the cheerful exclamation, "So you see how things still
manage to connect!" Throughout his long life, Forster always
believed in the inherent superiority of human relationships over
"the outer life of telegrams and anger."[42] His last years at
King's were devoted to strengthening the many ties of affection
in his own life. His friend Joe Ackerley has given the clearest
assessment of the meaning of Forster's final years at Cambridge:

> Bernard Shaw says somewhere, I think, that old men are danger-
> ous because they cease to care; Morgan lived to a great age, but he
> never grew old excepting in his body in the last few years of his
> life, he never became a blimp or a bore, the scientific age was not
> to his taste but he never ceased to care about the state of the
> world, and he never lost his faith in human values and human
> relationships. In the perennial freshness and adaptability of his
> mind he was perfectly able to keep up with the young, indeed one
> may say he outstripped them.[43]

conclusion

Soon after his arrival at Chhatarpur in 1923, Joe Ackerley was taken aside and given some friendly advice by an Anglo-Indian woman. He was told:

> "You know you gave us all a bit of a shock here at the first kick-off. You didn't introduce yourself. That isn't done in India. You ought to have labelled yourself at once—we all have labels out here, so that we know where we are, so to speak; so you should have told us all about yourself at once—where you come from, your parents, school, 'varsity, profession, business, and so on. But you didn't. You just sat still and left us guessing, and that creates a bad impression. . . . I thought I'd better warn you so that you'll know what's expected of you in the future."[1]

From this one gets a sharp image of the essentially ambiguous position of the English in India: their compulsion to label everything and everyone was an expression of their uncertain identity in an implacably alien land. Sensing this when he was in India, Forster symbolized it in the English plan to number the Marabar Caves with white paint—another futile attempt to classify the void, to render India slightly more congenial to Western notions of order. Like Fielding, whose aim is to "slink through India unlabelled,"[2] Forster tried to avoid being classified when he was there. Armed only with the vague humanist's creed of "kindness, kindness, and more kindness,"[3] he was determined not to be shut off from anything India might offer him. For Forster, the greatest failing of the British in India was that they had isolated themselves from the people they presumed to rule, an isolation which created only disharmony in human affairs. This is probably why Hinduism's emphasis on unity and reconciliation attracted him so powerfully, and in a 1959 talk he pointed to the central significance of this theme in his novel:

> For the book is not really about politics, though it is the political aspect of it that caught the general public and made it sell. It's about something wider than politics, about the search of the human race for a more lasting home, about the universe as embodied in the Indian earth and the Indian sky, about the horror lurking in the Marabar Caves and the release symbolised by the birth of Krishna. It is—or rather desires to be—philosophic and poetic. . . .[4]

The Gokul Ashtami festival proclaims that while individuals may be small in the grand scheme of the universe, they nevertheless have meaning. This is the antithesis of the message of the caves ("Everything exists, nothing has value"),[5] which suggests that "though people are important, the relations between them are not. . . ."[6]

Yet in *A Passage to India* Forster's humanism is more tentative than anywhere else in his writing—the image of Fielding and Adela Quested as "dwarfs shaking hands"[7] reveals the author in a distinctly gloomy mood. In the midst of writing the novel in 1923, Forster wrote despairingly to Syed Ross Masood:

> I am left with plenty of trusty acquaintances and relatives, but life is alarmingly empty in other respects, and no doubt will continue to empty itself as I grow older. All that remains positive is the expression of oneself through art and this at present I cannot attain to. Art seems the only true vent for our sorrows and for the dissatisfactions that are somehow more painful even than our sorrows. It alone redresses the bias against romance that runs through the material of the world. Personal relations succeed in this way less and less. It is my fault—not other people's. I bring less and less to them.[8]

Forster is at his most pessimistic here, but this is not the tone which dominates the end of the book: the clear-headed realism of the final encounter between Aziz and Fielding declares that the echo of the caves has been dispelled. Forster acknowledges the existence of evil in the world, but is not willing to admit its primacy. His description of personal affection as "little ineffectual unquenchable flames"[9] indicates his modest but definite hope for the future of human relations in India. In this aspect, *A Passage to India* is an affirmation, albeit a tenuous one, of the imperishability of the human spirit under even the worst of conditions.

appendix

Itinerary of Forster's First Visit to India, 1912–13

The following chronology has been constructed primarily from Forster's own diary, but The Hill *of* Devi *and P. N. Furbank's* E. M. Forster: A Life *have also been utilized to fill in the gaps. Forster was an assiduous diarist, but there is one large blank space (February 4–March 1, 1913) that remains a mystery.*

1912	October 7	Embarked from Naples on S. S. *City of Birmingham*
	October 8–21	At sea
	October 22	Arrive Bombay
	October 23–24	Bombay to Aligarh (via Agra)
	October 25–31	Aligarh
	November 1–2	Delhi
	November 3–6	Lahore
	November 7–9	Peshawar
	November 10–13	Lahore
	November 14–18	Simla
	November 19–24	Delhi, Agra
	November 25–27	Gwalior
	November 27	Gwalior to Chhatarpur (via Jhansi)
	November 28–	
	December 10	Chhatarpur
	December 11–19	Bhopal, Ujjain, Udaipur
	December 20–23	Indore
	December 24–	
1913	January 2	Dewas
	January 3	Dewas to Allahabad

January 4–6	Allahabad
January 6–10	Benares
January 11–27	Patna (Bankipore)
January 28	Barabar Caves
January 29	Gaya, Boddh Gaya
January 30	Sasaram, Allahabad
January 31–	
February 3	Allahabad
March 2	Lahore
March 3	Lahore to Patiala (via Amritsar)
March 4–6	Patiala
March 6–9	Delhi
March 10	Jaipur
March 11–16	Jodhpur
March 16–18	Mount Abu
March 19	Mount Abu to Bombay
March 20	Bombay to Hyderabad
March 21–23	Hyderabad
March 24–	
April 1	Aurangabad
April 2	Bombay (embarked in evening for England)

Notes

PREFACE

1. Selections from Forster's Indian diary appeared as "Indian Entries" in *Encounter* in January 1962, and were reprinted in *Harper's* a month later under the title "Indian Entries from a Diary" with an introduction by Santha Rama Rau.

2. I have used the term "Anglo-Indian" throughout to identify English people living and working in India. Beginning with the 1911 Census, "Anglo-Indian" designated those of mixed European and Indian parentage, but I have chosen to stay with Forster's own usage.

As for "English" and "British," I have used them interchangeably in the simple interests of variety. Some may be dismayed by my failure to distinguish between Scots, Irish, and English, but I saw no alternative in this troublesome matter.

I. THE BACKGROUND OF THE FIRST VISIT

1. Forster, *Marianne Thornton*, p. 277.
2. Howse, *Saints in Politics*, p. vii.
3. Quoted in Embree, *Charles Grant and British Rule*, p. 274.
4. Forster, "Missionaries," p. 545.
5. Forster, *Marianne Thornton*, pp. 278–79.
6. Forster, "A Presidential Address to the Cambridge Humanists," p. 2.
7. Forster, "Three Countries," Forster Typescripts, King's College Library, Cambridge, Ser. 2, vol. 1, p. 121.
8. Forster, *Marianne Thornton*, p. 301.
9. Colmer, *E. M. Forster*, p. 5.
10. Forster, "Notes on the English Character," in *Abinger Harvest*, p. 5.
11. Forster, *Goldsworthy Lowes Dickinson*, p. 22.
12. Quoted in Stone, *The Cave and the Mountain*, p. 63.
13. Forster, *Goldsworthy Lowes Dickinson*, p. 61.
14. Stone, *The Cave and the Mountain*, p. 67.
15. Forster, *Goldsworthy Lowes Dickinson*, pp. 29–30.
16. David Jones, "E. M. Forster on His Life and Books," p. 11.
17. Forster, "Three Countries," p. 125.

18. In 1920, the college achieved university status and became Aligarh Muslim University.

19. See deBary, ed., *Sources of the Indian Tradition*, II, 187–229.

20. David Lelyveld, *Aligarh's First Generation*, p. 302.

21. Ibid.

22. Not to be confused with the barrister Syed Mahmoud of Bankipore, who is mentioned in chapter 2.

23. This was actually the highest position in the judiciary that any Indian had achieved so far.

24. The geography of Chhatarpur State was to serve as a model for Mau in Part 3 of *A Passage to India* (see chapter 3 below) and the fantastical figure of the Maharajah was the primary inspiration for Godbole in the novel. The uncanny sequence of links does not end here, for Forster was instrumental in making arrangements in 1923 for his friend Joe Ackerley to go out to Chhatarpur as private secretary to the Maharajah (by then an old man). Out of Ackerley's experience there came his delightful *Hindoo Holiday*.

25. For a fuller account of Morison's career at Aligarh, see Lelyveld, *Aligarh's First Generation*.

26. Kidwai, ed., *Muraqqa-e-Masood* [Portrait of Masood], p. 4.

27. Ibid., p. 10.

28. For these letters, I am deeply indebted to Masood's widow, Begum Chhatari of Karachi (Pakistan), and also to the guardian of the Masood Papers, Jalil A. Kidwai.

29. E. M. Forster to Syed Ross Masood, 21 April 1907, Masood Papers.

30. Forster to Masood, 4 November 1908, ibid.

31. Forster to Masood, 15 November 1908, ibid.

32. Forster to Masood, 1 January 1909, ibid.

33. Forster to Masood, 30 December 1909, ibid. Efforts to locate the full text of this poem have proved unsuccessful.

34. Forster to Masood, 14 January 1910, ibid.

35. Forster, "Syed Ross Masood," in *Two Cheers for Democracy*, pp. 293–94.

36. Ibid., p. 292.

37. Ibid.

38. Forster to Masood, 21 November 1910, Masood Papers.

39. Forster to Masood, undated letter (clearly from 1911), ibid.

40. Forster to Masood, 4 February 1911, ibid.

41. Masood's career in law lasted less than a year: he hated the legal profession and when his application for the Indian Educational Service was accepted in 1913, he took a post as Headmaster of Government High School, Patna. Subsequently he had a distinguished career as an educator, serving as Director of Public Instruction of Hyderabad State from 1918 to 1929 and then as Vice-Chancellor of Aligarh Muslim University (founded by his grandfather) from 1929 to 1934.

II. FIRST PASSAGE: BRITISH INDIA, 1912–13

1. A fourth man, G. H. Luce, who was en route to a job in Burma, also accompanied them as far as Bombay, but both Forster's and Dickinson's diaries indicate that he kept entirely to himself during the voyage.

2. Dickinson and Trevelyan left Forster in Chhatarpur on December 10 to continue eastward to China, but Forster stayed in India for nearly four more months.

3. Forster, "Indian Diary," MS, King's College Library, Cambridge, p. 1. This will be referred to hereafter as "Indian Diary."

4. Ibid., p. 2.

5. Forster, *Goldsworthy Lowes Dickinson,* pp. 112–13.

6. Ibid.

7. Dickinson, *Autobiography,* p. 178.

8. "Indian Diary," p. 6.

9. Goldsworthy Lowes Dickinson, "Diary of Eastern Tour, 1912–13," MS, King's College Library, Cambridge, p. 5.

10. "Indian Diary," p. 7.

11. Dickinson, "Diary of Eastern Tour," p. 5.

12. Ibid.

13. Ibid., p. 6.

14. Greenberger, *The British Image of India,* p. 42.

15. Ackerley, *Hindoo Holiday,* pp. 97–98.

16. Cotton, *New India,* p. 31.

17. Dickinson, "Diary of Eastern Tour," p. 4.

18. "Indian Diary," p. 7.

19. Dickinson, *Autobiography,* p. 178.

20. The *Quarterly Indian Army List* for April 1913 has the following entry for Searight: "Searight, A. K. (Lieutenant), The Queen's Own (Royal West Kent Regiment), Peshawar. First Command 2 March 1904/Regiment 12 October 1907."

21. Forster, *A Passage to India: The Everyman Edition,* p. 142. All further references will be to this edition, which will be called simply *Passage.*

22. "Indian Diary," pp. 10–11. Forster, Trevelyan, and Dickinson instead stayed at the Apollo Hotel, of which Dickinson remarked in his diary, "7 rupees [per] person—comfortable enough." Dickinson, "Diary of Eastern Tour," p. 6.

23. *Passage,* p. 182.

24. "Indian Diary," p. 11.

25. Ibid.

26. Forster did visit Ellora by himself later in his visit, in March 1913.

27. Forster, *Goldsworthy Lowes Dickinson,* p. 113.

28. *Passage,* p. 110.

29. Candler, *Youth and the East,* pp. 66–67.

30. *Passage,* p. 32.

31. From Olive Douglas, *Olive in India* (1913), quoted in Brown, *The Sahibs,* p. 212.

32. *Passage,* p. 5.

33. Ibid., p. 81.

34. His impressions of these places are only briefly noted in his diary and they seem not to have had any substantial impact on him. Benares, Allahabad, and Mount Abu, and Jaipur also evoked little response.

35. "Indian Diary," pp. 12–13.

36. *Passage*, p. 218.

37. Forster reached Lahore on November 3; Dickinson and Trevelyan, coming from Aurangabad, had arrived a day earlier.

38. "Indian Diary," p. 23.

39. Ibid., pp. 23–24.

40. Kipling's poems played a crucial role in shaping popular attitudes concerning manliness as a criterion for judging Indians and other "subject races." One of his most famous poems, "Fuzzy-Wuzzy" (written as a tribute to the Mahdi's forces, who had fought the British in the Sudan), contains perhaps his best-known expression of the belief in the ultimate supremacy of physical prowess:

So 'ere's to you, Fuzzy-Wuzzy, at your 'ome in the Sowdan;
You're a pore benighted 'eathen but a first-class fightin' man;
We gives you your certifikit, an' if you want it signed
We'll come an' 'ave a romp with you whenever yo're inclined.
From *Barrack-Room Ballads*, p. 9.

41. "Indian Diary," pp. 25–26.

42. *Passage*, p. 46.

43. "Indian Diary," p. 27.

44. Forster, *Goldsworthy Lowes Dickinson*, pp. 114–15. "Prairie oysters" are a concoction made of whiskey and raw egg yolk, topped with cayenne pepper and swallowed in one gulp.

45. "Indian Diary," p. 27. It should be noted that Forster's evening in Peshawar was a special occasion: usually, regimental mess was a grim and dreary affair which officers were required to attend night after night. One lifelong observer of the British in India contends that the monotony of regimental mess may account for some of the curious marriages by Army officers: "During the monsoon one would arrive more or less soaked, but there was no reprieve from this ancient and tiresome ritual. Only in marriage, which permitted an officer to dine at home, was there relief from this nightly torture. I often thought that it was an overriding factor in persuading a man to take the plunge; how otherwise account for some of the strange alliances one frequently came across in British India?" Morris, *Eating the Indian Air*, p. 47.

46. "Indian Diary," p. 26.

47. Ibid., p. 31.

48. One of Kipling's Anglo-Indian ladies complains, "It is impossible to start a *salon* in Simla. A bar would be much more to the point." From "The Education of Otis Yeere" in *Under the Deodars*, p. 5.

49. Leonard Woolf, *Growing*, p. 46.

50. Forster, "The Poems of Kipling," MS, King's College Library, Cambridge, p. 13.

51. *Passage*, p. 224.

52. Duncan had married Everard Charles Cotes in 1892: in 1912, when Forster met him, Cotes was the Managing Director of the Associated Press of Simla and the Eastern News Agency. See *Thacker's Indian Directory—1914*, p. 84.

53. "Indian Diary," p. 31.

54. Ibid., pp. 29–30. A somewhat longer version of this appeared in *Abinger Harvest* as "Advance, India!" It is noteworthy that the latter account, based upon the diary entry but written some two years later, is less critical and ends on a vaguely positive note by acknowledging the courage of the two families in attempting to introduce innovation in an essentially conservative cultural setting.

55. *Passage*, p. 33.

56. Masood's return to India in February 1912 after his Oxford career prompted a flattering editorial in the militant Muslim weekly *Comrade* (edited by Mohammed Ali) entitled "Masood's 'Hereditary Duties'." It pointed to the legacy of "the Sage of Aligarh" and expressed confidence in the readiness of the sage's grandson to carry on the family tradition of service to the Indian Muslim community. See Kidwai, ed., *Khayaban-e-Masood*, pp. 15–16.

57. Dickinson, "Diary of Eastern Tour," p. 23. Leonard Woolf had much the same complaint when he served in Ceylon as a magistrate: "every case is an intricate tangle of lies, for even if a man has a true case, he always buys witnesses who have never seen the thing take place, and answers your questions as he thinks that you want them answered." Leonard Woolf to R. C. Trevelyan, Jaffna, 28 May 1905, Trevelyan Papers.

58. Dickinson, "Diary of Eastern Tour," p. 22.

59. *Passage*, p. 31. " 'They ought never to have been allowed to drive in; it's so bad for them.' "

60. Ibid., p. 29. " 'What do you think of the Aryan brother in a topi and spats?' "

61. Ibid., p. 39.

62. Ibid., p. xxix.

63. Buchanan-Hamilton, *Journal*, pp. 174–75, 178.

64. Dickinson, "Diary of Eastern Tour," p. 22. The single large street that both Dickinson and Buchanan-Hamilton refer to is today called "Ashok Raj Path." It connects the old British civil lines at Bankipore with the congested center-city area known as Patna City.

65. *Passage*, p. 1.

66. This hospital is very likely an early forerunner of what is now Patna Medical College Hospital, located about half a mile east of the maidan (today called Gandhi Maidan). See Kumar, *Bihar District Gazetteers: Patna*, pp. 554–55.

67. *Passage*, pp. 1–2.

68. "Indian Diary," p. 57.

69. Forster to Trevelyan, Bankipore, 21 January 1913, Trevelyan Papers.

70. "Indian Diary," p. 57. In the novel, Aziz warns Mrs. Moore when he first meets her, " 'I think you ought not to walk at night alone, Mrs. Moore. There are bad characters about and leopards may come across from the Marabar Hills. Snakes also.' " (p. 13)

71. W. G. Archer has proposed that Mahmoud was very likely the source of information concerning the trial scene in *A Passage to India*. Since Patna had become the capital of the newly created province of Bihar in 1912, it possessed by the time of Forster's visit a formidable hierarchy which would have made the blatant interference by the Anglo-Indian community in the trial scene impossible. Dr. Archer offers an authoritative suggestion as to the source of that all-important scene: "I myself knew Syed Mahmoud well and once discussed with him Forster's visit to Patna. He agreed that the trial scene could not have happened in Patna in the 1910s and 20s, but he did say that it was not uncommon for members of the planter community in North Bihar (i.e. on the other side of the Ganges from Patna in places such as Chapra and Muzaffarpur) to descend on a court, plant themselves on the rostrum beside a magistrate and thus intimidate him. This might happen in cases where a particular planter was accused of 'taking the law into his own hands' and hence was a form of protecting the 'Planter's Raj,' as it was called." (Letter to the author, 26 September 1978.)

72. I am indebted to Dr. Archer for pointing out the connection between Forster's visit to the caves and his acquaintance with Jackson. Dr. Archer also speculates that Jackson might have been the model for Fielding: both men were schoolmasters (and Jackson later became Principal of Patna College); their ages were rather close (Fielding is "over forty," while Jackson was thirty-eight in 1913); and Fielding was prevented from journeying to the caves (as Jackson did so often in 1913) only by a last-minute muddle involving Professor Godbole's *puja*.

73. Quoted in Kincaid, *British Social Life in India*, p. 240.

74. Greenberger, *The British Image of India*, p. 46.

75. Nirad C. Chaudhuri, "Passage To and From India," p. 73.

76. Ibid., p. 71.

77. Forster, "A Known Indian."

78. Natwar-Singh, ed., *E. M. Forster: A Tribute*, p. xii.

79. Sen, ed., *Dictionary of National Biography*, III, 148–50.

80. "Indian Diary," p. 20. The money Masood referred to was the fund for a new Muslim university. It should be noted that by 1912, Mohammed Ali had not yet attained his fullest measure of fame. As the Great War approached in Europe, Mohammed Ali and his older brother Shaukat Ali became leaders of the anti-British agitation over Whitehall's unabashed and open hostility toward Turkey. The Ali brothers were seen as a direct threat to the Government of India once the war broke out in 1914, and the two were interned from early 1915 until 1919. In the 1920s, both remained active in Muslim politics: Mohammed Ali was central in the founding of the new Muslim university, the *Jamia Millia Islamia* (first at Aligarh, and then at Delhi) in 1920, while Shaukat Ali was a key figure in the Khilafat movement. An excellent account of the movement to establish a Muslim university is Minault and Lelyveld, "The Campaign for a Muslim University, 1898–1920."

81. An article entitled "The Balkan War and the Indian Musalmans" that appeared in the *Hindustan Review* of July 1913 offers a good example of the intense emotional involvement of the Indian Muslim community in this seemingly faraway conflict. The article gives a lucid account of the affair which indicates the high level of interest in this issue at the time. The *Hindustan Review* was

published in Patna by Sachchidananda Sinha, a prominent figure in the early independence movement in Bihar: Forster had met Sinha in January 1913 and had been quite impressed with him. Sinha's journal was one of the most intellectually sophisticated Indian periodicals in English at the time, publishing articles from a wide spectrum of viewpoints. Indeed, the article which is excerpted below appeared in the same issue with several pieces by Rabindranath Tagore:

> The Crescent in its glory is all but set in Europe and there is wailing in the tents of Ottoman and darkness over the whole of the Mohammedan world. . . . All throughout the war the Indian Musalmans identified themselves so closely with Turkey, as far as it was possible, that the war was bound to have a great effect on them for good or for evil. . . . And because Turkey was regarded as the sole surviving power of Islam, its only hope of glory, this revelation of its weakness was accompanied with all the bitterness of a present disappointment and the uncertainty of a gloomy future. It was such a grievous shock that it unnerved the whole Mohammedan world. . . . In India the public causes, with which the Mohammedan community concerned itself, suffered considerably on account of the war. . . . For example, one might say that the war for the time being practically killed the University movement. It was with some difficulty that the money contributed for University purposes, was saved from being lent or given away to Turkey, which would have meant the postponement of the University idea for many years to come.
>
> Hindustan Review, 28 (July 1913).

It is worth speculating on the authorship of this piece, which is signed only "An Indian Muslim." The scheme to donate to Turkey the money for the new university never really got beyond the planning stage, and since Syed Ross Masood was one of the principal organizers of the fund, it is quite possible that he was the author. Masood was living in Patna at the time and Sinha was a good friend of his. Furthermore, a comparison between this article and some of Masood's published English works reveals distinct similarities of style and voice. See, for instance, Masood's "How to Save the Great Muslim Culture?" in *Khayaban-e-Masood*.

82. Sen, ed., *Dictionary of National Biography*, I, 65–67. A valuable description of Ansari's home is provided by Halidé Edib, a Turkish woman who visited India in 1932. Edib was an active social reformer and advocate of women's rights who had met Ansari in 1913 when he led the Ansari Medical Mission to Turkey to provide medical and surgical aid to Turkish forces in the Balkan War. The following account testifies to Ansari's continued involvement in public life in the years after Forster met him:

> Dar-es-Salam is Dr. Ansari's residence. The name means House of Salam; also House of Islam. The spirit of Islam is broad enough to justify the name. But the house has its international and universal aspects as well. I was a guest for nearly two months. Salam House is a huge octagonal building of one storey, overlooking a square lawn. Cars move in and out along two straight parallel drives. A few steps lead up to the marble terrace, which runs the length of the facade. A profusion of red, white, and purple flowers in magenta-red pots are spread about, or twine themselves round the marble col-

umns of the terrace. The Congress flag waves overhead. It is an historical place; but to my mind its present significance is greater than its past. Mahatma Gandhi and Lord Irwin met there on a memorable occasion. At the time, the Parliamentary Board and the Shadow Cabinet also had their meetings there. The ancient, the mediaeval, and the modern come together: the ideas and aspirations of divergent personalities meet, coalesce, and the personalities disperse to set in motion new trends elsewhere. In the free India of the future, that house will be one of the principal landmarks in its making.

From Edib, *Inside India*, p. 27.

83. "Indian Diary," p. 20.
84. *Passage*, p. 43.
85. Ibid., pp. 63–64.
86. "Indian Diary," pp. 20–22.
87. *Passage*, p. 30.
88. Ibid., p. 89.
89. Indeed, Aligarh was sometimes referred to as "the Cambridge of India." See Lelyveld, *Aligarh's First Generation*, p. 218.
90. "Indian Diary," p. 14. The unsightly latrines in the college's inner courts were noticed by other visitors to Aligarh. The following description is taken from the accounts of visitors roughly contemporaneous with Forster:

In both quadrangles the sizable grounds around which these buildings sat were fitted out with gardens—and latrines. Latrines were poorly drained and overtaxed. Where a Cambridge college might be graced with a statue or fountain in the center of the quadrangle, Aligarh had an outhouse. The truth is, Aligarh was notable for its smell; the jails, someone said, were "sweeter."

(Lelyveld, *Aligarh's First Generation*, p. 165.)

It should be noted that although Forster makes frequent reference to unsanitary conditions in India in the early parts of his diary, as he becomes more at home in the country these comments virtually disappear. He never made the mistake of most Anglo-Indians (and of his friend Dickinson) of equating cleanliness with virtue.

91. "Indian Diary," p. 16.
92. Ibid., p. 15.
93. Ibid., p. 17.
94. Gaines, review of *A Passage to India*.

III. FIRST PASSAGE: PRINCELY INDIA, 1912–13

1. One Indian who spent many years as an administrator in Indore, a large princely state in central India, described the relationship between the princes and British Residents in these terms:

The princely states were all in theory sovereign states. But, as you know, theory and practice are not always the same. In fact, the princes could not lift a finger without the approval of the Government of India. . . . The Resident, who was supposed to be advising the prince, actually was there to look after him and make certain he didn't step out of line.
(Interview with K. G. Sharma, Indore, 16 June 1976.)

2. Lord, *The Maharajahs*, p. 64.

3. Kipling, "The Man Who Would Be King," in *Under the Deodars*, p. 193.

4. His full name and title was "His Highness Maharajah Vishvanath Singh Bahadur." When Forster met him, he was forty-six and had ruled Chhatarpur since the age of twenty-one. See Luard, *Chiefs and Leading Families in Central India*, p. 51.

5. Forster, *Goldsworthy Lowes Dickinson*, p. 115.

6. Natwar-Singh, ed., *E. M. Forster: A Tribute*, p. xii.

7. *Passage*, p. 59.

8. Braybrooke, ed., *The Ackerley Letters*, p. 8. The chronology of the writing of *A Passage to India* is important here. Chapters I–VII, which include the description of Godbole, were written c. 1913, after Forster had returned from his first visit to India. Except for a few scattered passages, the rest of the novel was composed between 1922 and 1924, after Forster's second Indian journey. Thus, the final section of the book ("Temple"), which portrays Godbole at the Gokul Ashtami festival, incorporates elements of both ceremonies and personalities that Forster had seen at Dewas in 1921. But the initial vision of Godbole stems directly from the author's 1912–13 visit, when he spent a good deal of time at Chhatarpur but only a few days at Dewas. See Oliver Stallybrass, "Forster's 'Wobblings': The Manuscripts of *A Passage to India*" in *Aspects of E. M. Forster*, pp. 148–49; also, Harrison, "The Manuscripts of *A Passage to India*."

9. *Passage*, p. 66. Both Godbole's name and his singing were borrowed from an evening Forster spent in Lahore with a Brahman named Godbole, who sang for him as they strolled through the public gardens. See Furbank, *E. M. Forster: A Life*, I, 249.

10. *Passage*, p. 18.

11. "Indian Diary," p. 43.

12. Forster, *Goldsworthy Lowes Dickinson*, p. 115.

13. Ibid.

14. Dickinson, *Autobiography*, p. 179.

15. Ibid., p. 180.

16. Ackerley, *Hindoo Holiday*, p. ix.

17. Dickinson, *Appearances*, pp. 18–20.

18. "Indian Diary," p. 42.

19. *Passage*, p. 265. The mention of the *saddhu* (holy man) who invoked the god's name "with comic results" is taken directly from one of the Krishna plays seen at Chhatarpur. Forster's diary takes note of "a comic Nativity story. Krishna steals the food of the Pundit who has come to congratulate his mother, for each time the Pundit says grace he [Krishna] heard Divinity invoked and had to come." ("Indian Diary," p. 42.)

20. Ibid., p. xxix.

21. Forster, *Goldsworthy Lowes Dickinson*, p. 223.
22. Ibid.
23. "Indian Diary," p. 35.
24. Ibid., p. 38.
25. *Passage*, p. xxix.
26. "Indian Diary," pp. 40–41.
27. *Passage*, pp. 267–68.
28. This incident is recounted by Sir Arthur Cunningham Lothian in *Kingdoms of Yesterday*, pp. 38–39.
29. Birdwood, *Khaki and Gown*, p. 40. Lothian also served in Nowgong as a young man: see *Kingdoms of Yesterday*, pp. 26–50.
30. "Indian Diary," p. 40.
31. Forster, *Goldsworthy Lowes Dickinson*, p. 115.
32. "Indian Diary," p. 42.
33. Ibid., p. 37.
34. Misra, *Ninth Annual Administration Report of the Chhatarpur State*, p. 44. A copy of this book is now in King's College Library, Cambridge among the books from Forster's personal library at Dewas in 1921. It contains the following inscription: "Presented to E. M. Forster Esq. by S. B. Misra with kind remembrances. Chhatarpur, Bundelkhand, Central India, 4-6-14."
35. *Passage*, p. 255.
36. "Indian Diary," p. 38.
37. *Passage*, p. 94.
38. Forster, "The Indian Mind" in *Albergo Empedocle and Other Writings*, p. 207.
39. Forster, *The Hill of Devi*, p. 8.
40. In a 1909 letter to Syed Ross Masood, Forster mentions seeing Darling: "I have just seen an I.C.S. friend from Dewas. I wish you could meet. He gives the most sympathetic account of your countrymen, while remaining a thorough Englishman himself. I think you would like him." Forster to Masood, 20 June 1909, Masood Papers.
41. This and the subsequent biographical information on the Rajah of Dewas Senior are taken from Malgonkar, *The Puars of Dewas Senior*, pp. 266–70.
42. The marriage, however, was not a happy one and the reverberations from its breakup in 1914 eventually led to the downfall of the Rajah in the late 1920s. See chapter 5 for a fuller discussion of this topic.
43. Malgonkar, *The Puars of Dewas Senior*, p. 275.
44. Forster, *The Hill of Devi*, pp. 31–32.
45. It is interesting to note that when Forster lived in Dewas in 1921 he usually wore Indian clothes and to this day is remembered there for having done so.
46. Forster, *The Hill of Devi*, pp. 35–36.
47. One of the most common ways of "going native" was to reject English food in favor of Indian cooking. Forster most certainly enjoyed Indian food and came to know it better as his Indian hosts along the way introduced him to new dishes. As for English cooking in India, it was for the most part as little understood and as badly prepared in Forster's time as it is today. The description of a

typical Anglo-Indian meal in *A Passage to India* (p. 37) is devastatingly accurate and gives one a good idea of the author's contempt, no doubt gained through unhappy experience, of English food in India:

> to dinner came Miss Derek and the McBrydes, and the menu was: Julienne soup full of bullety bottled peas, pseudo-cottage bread, fish full of branching bones, pretending to be plaice, more bottled peas with the cutlets, trifle, sardines on toast: the menu of Anglo-India. A dish might be added or subtracted as one rose or fell in the official scale, the peas might rattle less or more, the sardines and the vermouth be imported by a different firm, but the tradition remained; the food of exiles, cooked by servants who did not understand it.

48. Ackerley, *Hindoo Holiday*, pp. 81–82.
49. Forster, *The Hill of Devi*, p. 37.
50. Darling, *Apprentice to Power*, p. 142.
51. Forster, *The Hill of Devi*, pp. 29–30.
52. Ibid., pp. 55–56.
53. Ibid., pp. 40–41.
54. "Indian Diary," p. 45.
55. Rodney W. Jones, *Urban Politics in India*, pp. 24–27.
56. See Fitze, *Twilight of the Maharajahs*, p. 89.
57. *Passage*, p. 2.
58. For this and the subsequent information on the location of the Residency Club, I am most indebted to the keen memory and careful detective work of Dr. Reuben Moses of Indore Christian College.
59. Today the original Residency Club building is the home of the Agent of the State Bank of India's Indore branch. Most of its original features have been obscured by the prefabricated bank offices that are attached to it, but the pillared entrance and the low stone walls are still there, as well as sections of the original semicircular driveway.
60. Forster, *The Hill of Devi*, p. 25.
61. The history of Indore's clubs offers instructive parallels to the changing racial attitudes of both Indians and English in the period leading up to Indian independence in 1947. Since the nineteenth century, the Residency Club had been in operation to serve the social needs of the Anglo-Indian community in Indore; in Forster's time, it was flourishing, as were three clubs for Indians—the Officers' Club, the Yeshwant Cricket Club, and the Ladies' Club. In 1926, Maharajah Tukoji Rao III abdicated in favor of his son Yeshwant Rao II, then a student at Oxford: when the young man returned to Indore for the abdication ceremony, he was incensed to discover that the Residency Club still forbade Indian members. He accordingly made plans for a new Indian club much grander than the Residency Club, and in 1926 laid the foundation stone before returning to Oxford to resume his studies. When he came home in 1933 to assume full powers as an adult, this new club, called the Yeshwant Club, was formally dedicated. The three Indian clubs were consolidated into this new and most lavish one, which was run along English lines as a "mixed club," with the Maharajah's state officials bringing their wives along with them for the first time, on direct orders from the ruler. The Residency Club, meanwhile, remained closed to Indians until 1941, when circumstances intervened to make the old policy un-

tenable. In that year, the Residency Club temporarily became an Army Officers' Training School, and the daily presence of Indian officers in the club led to their being named honorary members; when the war ended and Indian independence seemed inevitable, these Indian officers were made full members. Thus, it was only at the last possible moment that Indians were admitted to the club which Forster had in mind when he created the Chandrapore Club. (For the above information, I am extremely grateful to Major M. M. Jagdale of Indore, who was one of the young officers who became the first Indian members of the Residency Club.)

Today, the irony of the changing fortunes of England and India is apparent in Indore's two clubs: the Yeshwant Club flourishes in spacious grounds, while the Residency Club has become a neglected and ill-attended club whose members told me that their only purpose in belonging was to use the single tennis court. The club building itself is extremely dilapidated, with only a ghostly and unused billiard room to remind one of its former status.

62. *Passage*, p. 53.

63. Ibid., p. 156. Children often served the purpose of taking everyone's minds off the crisis at hand. One English visitor recalls a situation similar to the one in the novel:

> I passed, one Christmas afternoon, through an Indian city which was thought to be on the verge of a serious anti-European outbreak, and all the Europeans were at the Club entertaining the children to a Christmas tree; so that those who would otherwise have been sitting home biting their nails in apprehension were devoting all their energies to persuading their offspring of the existence of Santa Claus.
>
> (Quoted in Brown, *The Sahibs*, p. 201.)

64. Ibid., p. 18.

65. Singh, *A Survey of Anglo-Indian Fiction*, p. 3.

66. "Indian Diary," p. 66. The Maharajah of Patiala at the time was Bhupinder Singh, an enormous man of lavish tastes and legendary sexual appetite. See Lord, *The Maharajahs*, pp. 157–64.

67. "Indian Diary," p. 65.

68. Ibid. Forster enjoyed riding horses and once wrote to Syed Ross Masood that he rode "with much pleasure and much incompetence." Forster to Masood, 3 May 1912, Masood Papers. For another, more significant ride that Forster took, see the section on Aurangabad.

69. Parry, *Delusions and Discoveries*, p. 162. Candler's Indian novels are: *A Vagabond in Asia* (1900); *The Mantle of the East* (1910); *The General Plan* (1911); *Siri Ram: Revolutionist* (1912); and *Abdication* (1922).

70. Forster, *Abinger Harvest*, p. 312.

71. Toy, *The Fortified Cities of India*, p. 81.

72. Fitzroy, *Courts and Camps in India*, p. 131.

73. "Indian Diary," p. 71.

74. *Passage*, p. 183.

75. Forster, *Abinger Harvest*, p. 313.

76. *The India Office List* (1912), p. 29. For a complete accounting of Goyder's career in India, see the 1933 *India Office List*, p. 634.

77. "Indian Diary," p. 73.

78. See Lord, *The Maharajahs,* pp. 66–87.

79. "Indian Diary," p. 80. The Char Minar (literally "four towers") is a monument in the center of Hyderabad that has become a symbol of the city's Muslim heritage. "May" is May Wylde, then Principal of Mahbubia Girls' College: Forster knew her through Maimie Aylward, who had married his father's cousin Inglis Synnot, and to whom Forster wrote many letters from India in 1912-13.

80. Ibid., p. 81.

81. Ibid., p. 82.

82. *Passage,* p. 235.

83. Abu Saeed Mirza was the youngest of the three Mirza brothers whom Forster knew. The eldest, Ahmed Mirza, served in the Nizam's public health department for many years, and Sajjad Mirza, the middle brother, was a noted barrister in Hyderabad. Their father was Moulvi Mohammed Aziz Mirza, once Home Secretary to the Nizam. I am most grateful to P. N. Furbank for helping me to identify the various.Mirzas and their careers.

84. "Indian Diary," pp. 85–86.

85. Ibid., pp. 84–85. The "Taj" referred to is the Bibi-ka-Makbara ("the Tomb of the Wife"), a smaller version of the Taj Mahal at Agra. The Emperor Aurangzeb sent architects to Agra around 1660 to study the Taj before building this mausoleum for his wife, Dil Ras Banu Begum. This tomb looks like the Taj at first glance, but closer inspection reveals less elaborate gardens and the predominant use of stucco in place of the Taj's luminous marble. For further information, see Siddiqui, *The Charm of Aurangabad.* Forster's diary records his initial visit to the place on the previous day: "Drive after tea to a comic edition of the Taj. Not bad at a distance, but proportions and materials are wrong" (p. 84).

86. "Indian Diary," p. 83.

87. *Passage,* p. 51.

88. Ibid., p. 58. Forster's notes to the Everyman edition of the novel are explicit as to the origins of this building: "Fielding's Garden House stands or stood near Aurangabad" (p. xxix).

89. "Indian Diary," p. 84.

90. *Passage,* p. 188.

91. "Indian Diary," p. 89.

92. Forster, introduction to "Indian Entries," p. 20.

93. "Indian Diary," p. 93.

IV. TIMELESS INDIA: THE BARABAR CAVES

1. *Passage,* p. 105.

2. Ibid.

3. Ibid., pp. 105–6.

4. Ibid., p. 121.

5. Ibid., p. 62.

6. Ibid., p. 63.

7. Ibid., p. 68.

8. "Indian Diary," p. 59. The six-spot beetle, which Forster later learned was "unentomological" (*Passage*, p. xxix), appears early in the novel when Aziz warns Mrs. Moore at the mosque of the dangers of walking alone at night. Mentioning leopards and snakes, he goes on: " 'For example, a six-spot beetle,' he continued. 'You pick it up, it bites, you die' " (p. 13).

9. *Passage*, pp. 120–21.

10. Ibid., pp. 106–7.

11. Buchanan-Hamilton also surveyed and described Patna: see the section on Forster's visit to Patna.

12. Buchanan-Hamilton, *Journal*, p. 11.

13. Ibid., pp. 16–17. There are several fine photographs of the Barabar Caves in Stone, *The Cave and the Mountain*, plates 28–30.

14. See P.C. Roy Chaudhury, *Bihar District Gazetteers: Gaya*, pp. 306–9. Also, Diwakar, *Bihar Through the Ages*, pp. 250–51; and Houlton, *Bihar: The Heart of India*, p. 40. These three accounts of the Barabar Caves all agree on the date of the principal caves (third century B.C.), pointing to the Ashokan inscriptions as evidence.

15. *Passage*, pp. 126–27.

16. Furbank, *E. M. Forster: A Life*, I, 248.

17. *Passage*, p. 182.

18. Ibid., p. 180.

19. Santha Rama Rau remembers that Forster once told her, "Mrs. Moore was always a rather tiresome old woman." Quoted in Natwar-Singh, *E. M. Forster: A Tribute*, p. 52.

20. *Passage*, p. 129.

21. Ibid., p. 180.

22. Forster, *Two Cheers for Democracy*, p. 70.

23. "Indian Diary," p. 91.

24. Perhaps the best critical study presenting the message of the caves as triumphant is Crews, *The Perils of Humanism*. See chapter 5 for a discussion of the Krishna festival at Mau and its function in the novel as an affirmation of human purpose.

V. SECOND PASSAGE: DEWAS, 1921

1. Stallybrass, *Aspects of E. M. Forster*, pp. 148–49.

2. Forster, "Three Countries," Forster Typescripts, King's College Library, Cambridge, ser. 2, vol. 1, p. 127.

3. Ibid.

4. See the chronology in Thomson's edition of *Albergo Empedocle*, p. 272.

5. The "modern wedding" viewed at Simla (see chapter 2) appeared in *New Weekly* (vol. 1), 11 April 1914, p. 106 as "Adrift in India, 2: Advance India!" (later included in *Abinger Harvest*). An expanded version of his observations on

Jodhpur was published as "Adrift in India, 3: In Rajasthan" in *New Weekly* (vol. 1), 16 May 1914, pp. 269–70 (also in *Abinger Harvest*). See Kirkpatrick, *A Bibliography of E. M. Forster*, and McDowell, *E. M. Forster: An Annotated Bibliography of Writings About Him.*

6. See Stone, *The Cave and the Mountain*, p. 282, and Colmer, *E. M. Forster*, p. 144.

7. A sizable number of letters from Forster to Masood written from Alexandria are currently in the possession of Masood's widow, but they were not available to me.

8. See Forster, *The Hill of Devi*, pp. 22 and 97.

9. See Malgonkar, *The Puars of Dewas Senior*, p. 274.

10. Forster, *The Hill of Devi*, p. 80.

11. Ibid., p. 81.

12. Ibid., p. 8.

13. Forster to Masood, 18 February 1921, Masood Papers. In the back of Forster's diary from 1912–13 are two pages headed "4/3/21—Second Voyage," which are a brief record of the first five days of the passage on the S. S. *Morea*. The first entry is from Tilbury Docks and merely notes the ship's departure, while the final one (dated March 8) is an unflattering description of Gibraltar. After this point, there are no more entries, but it seems that Forster did keep another diary at Dewas from which he constructed *The Hill of Devi*, also utilizing certain letters to his family in England.

14. Forster, *The Hill of Devi*, p. 89.

15. Ibid., pp. 86–87.

16. Ibid., pp. 98–99.

17. Ibid., p. 115.

18. Forster, "Woodlanders on Devi." Written in 1939, this statement of course alludes to the ultimate perversion of Western notions of order, Nazi Germany.

19. Forster, *The Hill of Devi*, p. 109. Forster is having fun here with the Hindu fondness for multiple manifestations of a single deity: Vishnu often appears in the form of a tortoise, and Krishna himself is an avatar of Vishnu.

20. Ibid. This particular method of assuring hygienic milk turns up in the last part of the novel as an item on the list of demands submitted by the Political Agent on tour in Mau.

21. *Passage*, p. 98.

22. Forster, *The Hill of Devi*, p. 65. Writing of the Maharajah's later financial troubles with the British, Forster, perhaps a bit naïvely, attributes the bitter feelings to a lack of consideration on the part of British officials. He describes Malcolm Darling's vain attempts to settle the matter amicably: "Malcolm interceded on his [the Maharajah's] behalf with various officials, high and low, and pointed out to them the importance, in such a case as this, of kindness and sympathy. There had been plenty of rectitude over the Dewas Senior bankruptcy, but no imagination and scant courtesy. . . . They listened—preferably down a telephone—but they knew they had behaved correctly, so had nothing to say. They were impeccably right and absolutely wrong." Forster, *The Hill of Devi*, pp. 259–60.

23. *Passage*, pp. 212–13.

24. Darling, *Apprentice to Power*, p. 39.
25. *Passage*, p. 12.
26. Forster, *The Hill of Devi*, p. 150.
27. *Passage*, pp. xxix–xxx.
28. An official British listing of major Indian religious holidays (dated 1914) contains this information on the festival:

This is the anniversary of the day of the birth of Çrī Kṛṣṇa at Mathurā. This festival is observed on the eighth lunar day in the dark fortnight of the month of Bhādra (August–September) in Upper India or of Çrāvaṇa (July–August) in the South and Bombay, and is one of the most important of the fasts observed by all Hindus, especially by the followers of Viṣṇu, throughout India. It is worthy of note that it is not neglected by the followers of Çiva, or by those of any other sect. Abstinence is practised on the day previous and on the day itself rigid fast is observed by all pious followers of Viṣṇu and also by other Hindus. Viṣṇu is worshipped in the form of Çrī Kṛṣṇa at midnight, when he was born.

An Alphabetical List, p. 41.

Readers of both the novel and *The Hill of Devi* will recognize features of the Dewas version in this generalized description, notably the fasting and the culmination of the adoration of Krishna at midnight.

29. Forster, *The Hill of Devi*, p. 178.
30. *Passage*, pp. 247–48.
31. In *The Hill of Devi*, this is described on p. 169; in the novel, on p. 271.
32. This is on pp. 166–67 of *The Hill of Devi*; in the novel, on pp. 252–53.
33. Levine, *Creation and Criticism*.
34. Forster, *The Hill of Devi*, p. 170.
35. *Passage*, pp. 274–75. I have restored the correct reading of the line: "Others praised him *with* attributes . . ." in accordance with the Abinger edition of the novel.
36. Ibid., p. 276.
37. Ibid., p. 253.
38. Spencer, "Hinduism in *A Passage to India*," p. 286.
39. *Passage*, p. 128.
40. Ibid., pp. 249–50.
41. Ibid., p. 28.
42. Ibid., p. 129.
43. Ibid., p. 189.
44. Forster, "A Presidential Address to the Cambridge Humanists," pp. 6–7.
45. *Passage*, p. 252. In his diary of the 1912–13 visit, Forster reveals the origin of "God si love": "At Moghul Serai station: Right is might, Might is right. Time is money. God si love. In block letters on marble blocks." "Indian Diary," p. 56.
46. Forster, "A Presidential Address to the Cambridge Humanists," p. 7.
47. Forster, "The Poems of Kipling," pp. 14–15.
48. Forster, *The Hill of Devi*, p. 266.
49. *Passage*, p. 279.

50. Forster, *The Hill of Devi*, pp. 159–60.

51. Forster, "The Temple," *Athenaeum*, 26 September 1919, p. 947.

52. Forster, *The Hill of Devi*, p. 169.

53. Interview with Sardar A.A. Partil Chalukey, Dewas, 20 June 1976.

54. Forster, *The Hill of Devi*, pp. 100–102.

55. Ibid., pp. 99–100.

56. As Forster noted near the end of *The Hill of Devi*, his time at Dewas was also artistically confining. He described his inability to add to the early chapters of his novel begun eight years earlier: "I used to look at them of an evening in my room at Dewas, and felt only distaste and despair. The gap between India remembered and India experienced was too wide." Forster, *The Hill of Devi*, p. 238.

57. Forster, *The Hill of Devi*, p. 235.

58. *Passage*, p. 12.

59. Ibid.

60. Syed Ali Akbar, "E. M. Forster in India" in *The Illustrated Weekly of India*, 18 October 1970, p. 25.

61. Ibid. Syed Ali Akbar suggests that two placenames here were adopted by Forster for his novel, "Gungawati" and "Mudgal." It is the Gangavati road that Ronny Heaslop orders the Nawab Bahadur's driver to avoid (p. 72), and Miss Derek is employed by Mudkul State (p. 75). Syed Ali Akbar's contention seems quite plausible, as both names appear for the first time in portions of the novel written after the 1921 journey.

62. *Passage*, p. 166.

63. Ibid., pp. 166–67.

64. In later editions, Forster added the name of the Maharajah of Dewas to the dedication. See the author's note on p. 238 of *The Hill of Devi*.

65. *Passage*, p. 8.

66. Kidwai, *Muraqqa-e-Masood*, p. 34. Like Aziz, Masood also wrote poetry constantly.

67. Interview with H. C. Dhanda, Indore, 20 June 1976. Dhanda grew up in Indore, where a childhood playmate was Amtul Raschid, daughter of Mohammed Abdul Raschid, then Minister of Law of Holkar State (Indore): she later became the second wife of Syed Ross Masood and is now living in Karachi, having remarried a member of the illustrious Chhatari family of Aligarh. Dhanda, after serving in Bhopal (where he worked closely with Masood), returned to Indore, where he was in charge of Labor and Industrial Affairs during the Second World War; in 1947 he served briefly as Deputy Prime Minister of Holkar State in the next-to-last cabinet before Indian independence. He is now a prominent barrister in Indore.

68. Kidwai, *Muraqqa-e-Masood,* p. 33.

69. *Passage*, p. 138.

70. Forster, *Two Cheers for Democracy*, p. 294.

71. *Passage*, p. 233.

72. The correspondence between Masood and Syed Mahmoud of Bankipore, whom Forster met in 1913, offers further insights into Masood's character. These letters, now in the Nehru Memorial Museum in New Delhi, reveal Masood as an extremely volatile person who fluctuated, sometimes wildly, between

moods of lavish affection and sharp hostility. His relationship with Syed Mahmoud was complicated by the labyrinthine political quarrels among Indian Muslims at the time, but the correspondence nevertheless constitutes a record of a friendship which seems to have been at the mercy of Masood's ever-changing moods. Aziz also has in him this streak of utter unpredictability. I am grateful to the Head of the Research and Publications Division of the Nehru Museum, Dr. D. N. Panigrahi, for making this material available to me.

VI. RETURN TO INDIA, 1945

1. Forster, "Three Countries," in Forster Typescripts, King's College Library, Cambridge, ser. 2, vol. 1, pp. 127–28.
2. See Forster, *The Hill of Devi*, p. 238.
3. Forster to Elizabeth (Bessie) Trevelyan, 10 June 1926, Trevelyan Papers.
4. Horne, "Letter to the Editor" in *New Statesman*, 16 August 1924. Other reviews in England had been cautiously favorable: one of the best, understandably, was Leonard Woolf's review in *Nation and Athenaeum* of 14 June 1924.
5. Horne, "Letter to the Editor."
6. Fitzroy, *Courts and Camps in India*, p. 213. Forster mentions in *The Hill of Devi* that his novel was "ill thought of" by Lord and Lady Reading, who made the mistake of criticizing it at a dinner attended by the Maharajah of Dewas, who, as Forster gleefully notes, calmly let them finish and then "proceeded to praise the work warmly" (p. 243).
7. Quoted in Gardner, ed., *Critical Heritage*, p. 290.
8. Horne, "Letter to the Editor."
9. K. Natwar Singh, "Only Connect . . . E. M. Forster and India" in Gowda, ed., *A Garland for E. M. Forster*, p. 111.
10. *Passage*, p. 282.
11. Forster, *The Hill of Devi*, p. 237.
12. Forster, "Reflections in India. I. Too Late?" and "Reflections in India. II. The Prince's Progress."
13. Forster, "India and the Turk."
14. Brander, *E. M. Forster*, p. 14.
15. Interview with Begum Amtul Chhatari, Karachi, 10 July 1976. Begum Chhatari told me that she always called Forster "Forscha," a combination of his name and the Hindustani word *chacha*, meaning "uncle."
16. This piece was later published in *Two Cheers for Democracy* as "Syed Ross Masood."
17. Forster, "Sir Tukoji Rao Puar."
18. *Broadcast Talks by E. M. Forster* (including "We Speak to India: Some Books"), Forster Typescripts, King's College Library, Cambridge, ser. 1, vol. 22 (1930–43) and vol. 23 (1944–60).

19. Forster, "Indian Photographic Exhibition," broadcast on BBC Eastern Service on 22 November 1940, Forster Typescripts, ser. 1, vol. 22, pp. 97–98.

20. Isherwood, *Down There on a Visit*, p. 162.

21. The acronym PEN stands for "poets, playwrights, editors, essayists, novelists."

22. Forster, "India Again" in *Two Cheers for Democracy*, p. 319.

23. Ibid., pp. 319–20.

24. Ibid., pp. 320–21.

25. Ibid., p. 320.

26. Ibid., pp. 321–22.

27. E. M. Forster to R. C. Trevelyan, 26 November 1945, Trevelyan Papers. See the opening section of chapter 2 above for the description of Forster's arrival at Bombay in 1912.

28. Ibid.

29. See Akbar, "E. M. Forster in India," p. 27.

30. Forster, *The Hill of Devi*, p. 8.

31. Forster, "India Again" in *Two Cheers for Democracy*, p. 328.

32. Ibid.

33. See Stallybrass, *Aspects of E. M. Forster*, p. 22.

34. From 1945 to 1953, Forster actually lived in two rooms in a house at 3 Trumpington Street belonging to Patrick Wilkinson, a classical scholar who was then a Fellow of King's. In 1953, Forster moved to a set of rooms in the college itself and lived there until his death in 1970. See Stallybrass, *Aspects of E. M. Forster*, pp. 22–23 and Furbank, *E. M. Forster: A Life*, II, 263 ff.

35. Forster, "Message to India," broadcast on BBC Eastern Service on 15 August 1947, Forster Typescripts, ser. I, vol. 23, p. 441.

36. Major Deolekr told me that he found Forster every bit as personable and kind in London as he was in Dewas in 1921, when Deolekr was a frightened young man in his first post: "He was always extremely kind: a very considerate man. And so pleasant to work for—he treated me well, though I was only a foolish boy then." Interview with Major Sardar Deolekr, Dewas, 20 June 1976.

37. Forster, *The Hill of Devi*, p. 253.

38. Typescript of program note for opening night of Santha Rama Rau's play *A Passage to India* at the Oxford Playhouse on 19 January 1960, Santha Rama Rau Papers.

39. *Passage*, p. xxx.

40. An excellent article on Forster's later years at Cambridge is Panter-Downes, "Profile: Kingsman."

41. Letter from Forster to Ahmed Ali dated 24 December 1963, in the possession of the recipient. The book referred to is *E. M. Forster: A Tribute*, edited by K. Natwar-Singh. "The Buckinghams" are Bob and May Buckingham, with whom Forster often visited: it was at their house in Coventry (the one mentioned in this letter) that he died on 7 June 1970 at the age of ninety-one. I am most grateful to Ahmed Ali for permission to quote from this letter.

42. Forster, *Howards End*, p. 174.

43. Ackerley, *E. M. Forster—A Portrait*, p. 12.

CONCLUSION

1. Ackerley, *Hindoo Holiday,* p. 17.
2. *Passage,* p. 151.
3. Ibid., p. 99.
4. Forster, "Three Countries," in Forster Typescripts, King's College Library, Cambridge, ser. 2, vol. 1, p. 128.
5. *Passage,* p. 128.
6. Ibid., pp. 115–16.
7. Ibid., p. 229.
8. Forster to Masood, 23 May 1923, Masood Papers. This passage is very similar to one in the novel where Adela Quested wonders, " 'What is the use of personal relationships when everyone brings less and less to them?' " *Passage,* p. 170.
9. *Passage,* p. 90.

Bibliography

UNPUBLISHED MATERIAL

Goldsworthy Lowes Dickinson Papers. King's College Library. Cambridge, England.

E. M. Forster Papérs. King's College Library. Cambridge, England.

Syed Ross Masood Papers. Private Collection. Karachi, Pakistan.

Santha Rama Rau Papers. Mugar Memorial Library, Boston University. Boston, Massachusetts.

R. C. Trevelyan Papers. Trinity College Library. Cambridge, England.

GENERAL WORKS

Ackerley, J. R. *E. M. Forster: A Portrait*. London: Ian McKelvie, 1970.

—— *Hindoo Holiday*. New York: Viking, 1932.

Akbar, Syed Ali. "E. M. Forster in India." *The Illustrated Weekly of India*, 18 October 1970, pp. 25–27.

Ali, Ahmed. *Twilight in Delhi*. London: Hogarth, 1940.

An Alphabetical List of the Feasts and Holidays of the Hindus and Muhammadans. Calcutta: Superintendent, Government Printing, India, 1914.

Beer, J. B. *The Achievement of E. M. Forster*. London: Chatto and Windus, 1962.

Birdwood, William Riddell (Field-Marshal Birdwood of Anzac

and Totnes). *Khaki and Gown: An Autobiography.* New York: Robert Speller and Sons, 1957.

Brander, Laurence. *E. M. Forster.* Lewisburg, Pa.: Bucknell University Press, 1968.

Braybrooke, Neville, ed. *The Ackerley Letters.* New York: Harcourt Brace Jovanovich, 1975.

Brown, Hilton, ed. *The Sahibs.* London: William Hodge and Sons, 1948.

Buchanan-Hamilton, Francis. *Journal of Francis Buchanan (afterwards Hamilton).* Ed. V. H. Jackson. Patna: Superintendent, Government Printing, Bihar and Orissa, 1925.

Butler, Iris. *The Viceroy's Wife: Letters of Alice, Countess of Reading, from India, 1921–25.* London: Hodder and Stoughton, 1969.

Candler, Edmund. *Youth and the East: An Unconventional Autobiography.* Edinburgh: Blackwood, 1924.

Chaudhuri, Nirad C. "Passage To and From India." In Andrew Rutherford, ed. *Twentieth Century Interpretations of A Passage to India.* Englewood Cliffs, N. J.: Prentice-Hall, 1970.

Chaudhury, P. C. Roy. *Bihar District Gazetteers: Gaya.* Patna: Secretariat Press, 1957.

Chirol, Sir Valentine. *Indian Unrest.* London: Macmillan, 1910.

Choudhary, Radhakrishna. *History of Bihar.* Patna: Motilal Banarsidass, 1958.

Colmer, John. *E. M. Forster: The Personal Voice.* London: Routledge and Kegan Paul, 1975.

Cornell, Louis L. *Kipling in India.* London: Macmillan, 1966.

Cotton, Sir Henry. *New India.* London: Kegan, Paul, Trench, Trübner, 1907.

Crews, Frederick C. *E. M. Forster: The Perils of Humanism.* Princeton: Princeton University Press, 1962.

Darling, Sir Malcolm. *Apprentice to Power: India 1904–1908.* London: Hogarth, 1966.

Das, G. K. *E. M. Forster's India.* London: Macmillan, 1977.

de Bary, W. Theodore, ed. *Sources of the Indian Tradition.* Volume II. New York: Columbia University Press, 1958.

Dickinson, Goldsworthy Lowes. *Appearances*. Garden City, N. Y.: Doubleday, Page, 1914.

—— *The Autobiography of G. Lowes Dickinson*. Ed. Dennis Proctor. London: Gerald Duckworth, 1973.

Diwakar, R. R. *Bihar Through the Ages*. Calcutta: Orient Longmans, 1959.

Eapen, Karippacheril Chakko. "E. M. Forster and India." Ph.D. dissertation, University of Colorado, 1962.

Edib, Halidé. *Inside India*. London: Allen and Unwin, 1937.

Embree, Ainslie T. *Charles Grant and British Rule in India*. London: Allen and Unwin, 1962.

Fitze, Sir Kenneth. *Twilight of the Maharajahs*. London: John Murray, 1956.

Fitzroy, Yvonne. *Courts and Camps in India: Impressions of Vice-regal Tours, 1921–1924*. London: Methuen, 1926.

Forster, Edward Morgan. *Abinger Harvest*. 1936. Reprint, New York: Harcourt, Brace and World, 1964.

—— *Albergo Empedocle and Other Writings*. Ed. George H. Thomson. New York: Liveright, 1971.

—— *Goldsworthy Lowes Dickinson: The Abinger Edition*. London: Edward Arnold, 1973.

—— *The Hill of Devi*. New York: Harcourt, Brace and World, 1953.

—— *Howards End*. 1910. Reprint, New York: Vintage, 1921.

—— "India and the Turk." *Nation and Athenaeum*, 30 September 1922, pp. 844–45.

—— "Indian Entries." *Encounter* 18 (January 1962), 20–27. Also published as "Indian Entries from a Diary." Introduction by Santha Rama Rau. *Harper's* 224, (February 1962), 46–52.

—— "A Known Indian." Review of *A Passage to England* by Nirad C. Chaudhuri. *Observer*, 16 August 1959, p. 14.

—— *Marianne Thornton: A Domestic Biography, 1797–1887*. New York: Harcourt, Brace and World, 1956.

—— "Missionaries." *Athenaeum*, 22 October 1920, pp. 545–47.

—— *A Passage to India: The Everyman Edition*. 1924. Reprint, London: J. M. Dent and Sons, 1957.

—— "A Presidential Address to the Cambridge Humanists."
Bulletin of the University Humanist Foundation 11 (Spring
1963), 1–8.

—— "Reflections in India. I. Too Late?" *Nation and Athenaeum,* 21 January 1922, pp. 614–15.

—— "Reflections in India. II. The Prince's Progress." *Nation
and Athenaeum,* 28 January 1922, pp. 644–46.

—— "Sir Tukoji Rao Puar." *Times* (London), 28 December
1937, p. 14.

—— "The Temple." *Athenaeum,* 26 September 1919, p. 947.

—— *Two Cheers for Democracy.* 1938. Reprint, New York: Harcourt, Brace and World, 1951.

—— "Woodlanders on Devi." *New Statesman and Nation,*
6 May 1939, pp. 679–80.

Furbank, P. N. *E. M. Forster: A Life.* Volume I. *The Growth of
the Novelist (1879–1914).* Volume II. *Polycrates' Ring
(1914–1970).* London: Secker and Warburg, 1977–78.

Gaines, Clarence H. "Review of A Passage to India, by E. M.
Forster." *North American Review* 220 (December 1924), 375.

Gardner, Philip, ed. *E. M. Forster: The Critical Heritage.* London: Routledge and Kegan Paul, 1973.

Geddes, Patrick. *Town Planning Towards City Development: A
Report to the Durbar of Indore.* Indore: Holkar State Press,
1918.

Gowda, H. H. Anniah, ed. *A Garland for E. M. Forster.* Mysore:
The Literary Half-Yearly, 1969.

Greenberger, Allen J. *The British Image of India.* London: Oxford University Press, 1969.

Harrison, Robert L. "The Manuscripts of *A Passage to India.*"
Ph.D. dissertation, University of Texas, 1964.

Horne, E. A. "Letter to the Editor." *New Statesman* 23, no. 591
(16 August 1924), pp. 543–44.

Houlton, Sir John. *Bihar: The Heart of India.* Calcutta: Orient
Longmans, 1949.

Howe, Susanne. *Novels of Empire.* New York: Columbia University Press, 1949.

Howse, Ernest M. *Saints in Politics: The Clapham Sect and the*

Growth of Freedom. Toronto: University of Toronto Press, 1952.

Hutchins, Francis G. *The Illusion of Permanence: British Imperialism in India.* Princeton: Princeton University Press, 1967.

The India Office List, 1912. London: Harrison and Sons, 1912.

Isherwood, Christopher. *Down There on a Visit.* New York: Simon and Schuster, 1962.

Jones, David. "E. M. Forster on his Life and Books." *Listener* 61 (January 1959), 11–12.

Jones, J. P., ed. *The Year Book of Missions in India, Burma, and Ceylon—1912.* Madras: The Christian Literature Society for India, 1912.

Jones, Rodney W. *Urban Politics in India.* Berkeley: University of California Press, 1974.

Kidwai, Jalil A., ed. *Khayaban-e-Masood* [Flower-Garden of Masood]. Karachi: Ross Masood Education and Culture Society of Pakistan, 1970.

―― *Muraqqa-e-Masood* [Portrait of Masood]. Karachi: Ross Masood Education and Culture Society of Pakistan, 1966.

Kincaid, Dennis. *British Social Life in India.* London: George Rutledge and Sons, 1938.

Kipling, Rudyard. *Barrack-Room Ballads.* 1892. Reprint, New York: A. L. Burt, n.d.

―― *Kim.* New York: Macmillan, 1901.

―― *Plain Tales from the Hills.* New York: Macmillan, 1888.

―― *Under the Deodars.* 1890. Reprint, New York: Macmillan, 1913.

Kirkpatrick, B. J. *A Bibliography of E. M. Forster.* London: Rupert Hart-Davis, 1968.

Kumar, N. *Bihar District Gazetteers: Patna.* Patna: Government of Bihar, Gazetteers Branch, Revenue Department, 1970.

Lelyveld, David. *Aligarh's First Generation: Muslim Solidarity in British India.* Princeton: Princeton University Press, 1978.

Levine, June Perry. *Creation and Criticism: A Passage to India.* Lincoln: University of Nebraska Press, 1971.

Lewis, Robin Jared. "Orwell's *Burmese Days* and Forster's *A*

Passage to India: Two Novels of Human Relations in the British Empire." *Massachusetts Studies in English* 4, no. 3 (Spring 1974), 1–36.

Lord, John. *The Maharajahs.* New York: Random House, 1971.

Lothian, Sir Arthur Cunningham. *Kingdoms of Yesterday.* London: John Murray, 1951.

Luard, C. E. *Chiefs and Leading Families in Central India.* Calcutta: Superintendent, Government Printing, 1916.

Lynton, Harriet Ronken. *The Days of the Beloved.* Berkeley: University of California Press, 1974.

Macaulay, Rose. *The Writings of E. M. Forster.* New York: Harcourt Brace, 1938.

McDowell, Frederick P. W. *E. M. Forster.* New York: Twayne, 1969.

—— *E. M. Forster: An Annotated Bibliography of Writings About Him.* DeKalb, Ill.: Northern Illinois University Press, 1976.

Malgonkar, Manohar. *The Puars of Dewas Senior.* Bombay: Orient Longmans, 1963.

Minault, Gail, and David Lelyveld. "The Campaign for a Muslim University, 1898–1920." *Modern Asian Studies* 8, no. 2 (1974), 145–89.

Misra, Shyam Behari. *The Ninth Annual Administration Report of the Chhatarpur State, Bundelkhand, C. I. for Sambat 1969 (i.e. from 1st July 1912 to 30th June 1913).* Allahabad: Pioneer Press, 1914.

Morris, John. *Eating the Indian Air.* London: Hamish Hamilton, 1968.

Natwar-Singh, K., ed. *E. M. Forster: A Tribute.* New York: Harcourt, Brace and World, 1964.

O'Dwyer, Sir Michael. *India As I Knew It: 1885–1925.* London: Constable, 1925.

Panter-Downs, Mollie. "Profiles: Kingsman." *New Yorker* 35 (19 September 1959), 51–80.

Parry, Benita. *Delusions and Discoveries: Studies on India in the British Imagination, 1880–1930.* Berkeley: University of California Press, 1972.

The Quarterly Indian Army List for April 1913. Calcutta: Superintendent, Government Printing, India, 1913.

Rama Rau, Santha. *A Passage to India.* A play adapted from the novel by E. M. Forster. London: Edward Arnold, 1960.

Sen, S. P., ed. *Dictionary of National Biography.* 3 vols. Calcutta: Institute of Historical Studies, 1974.

Shahane, Vasant Anant. *E. M. Forster, A Reassessment.* Allahabad: Kitab Mahal, 1962.

Shrivastav, P. N. *Madhya Pradesh District Gazetteers: Indore.* Bhopal: Government Central Press, 1971.

Siddiqui, Safiuddin. *The Charm of Aurangabad.* Aurangabad: A.H.S. Mohamedbhoy, 1975.

Singh, Bhupal. *A Survey of Anglo-Indian Fiction.* 1934. Reprint, London: Curzon Press, 1974.

Spencer, Michael. "Hinduism in E. M. Forster's *A Passage to India.*" *Journal of Asian Studies* 27 (February 1968), 281–95.

Stallybrass, Oliver, ed. *Aspects of E. M. Forster.* New York: Harcourt, Brace and World, 1969.

Stone, Wilfred. *The Cave and the Mountain: A Study of E. M. Forster.* Stanford: Stanford University Press, 1966.

Thacker's Indian Directory—1914. Calcutta: Thacker Spink, 1914.

Toy, Sidney. *The Fortified Cities of India.* London: Heinemann, 1965.

—— *The Strongholds of India.* London: Heinemann, 1957.

Trilling, Lionel. *E. M. Forster.* 1943. Reprint, New York: New Directions, 1964.

Weston, Christine. *Indigo.* London: Collins, 1944.

Wilde, Alan. *Art and Order: A Study of E. M. Forster.* New York: New York University Press, 1964.

Woolf, Leonard. *Diaries in Ceylon, 1908–1911: Records of a Colonial Administrator.* Colombo: The Ceylon Historical Journal, 1962.

—— *Growing: An Autobiography of the Years 1904–1911.* London: Hogarth, 1961.

Index